Money Making Skills

Create a Stream of Income with Your Writing Skills

(The Ultimate Teen Guide to Personal Finance and Making Cents of Your Dollars)

James Meek

Published By **Barry Ackles**

James Meek

All Rights Reserved

Money Making Skills: Create a Stream of Income with Your Writing Skills (The Ultimate Teen Guide to Personal Finance and Making Cents of Your Dollars)

ISBN 978-1-7382957-7-7

No part of this guidebook shall be reproduced in any form without permission in writing from the publisher except in the case of brief quotations embodied in critical articles or reviews.

Legal & Disclaimer

The information contained in this book is not designed to replace or take the place of any form of medicine or professional medical advice. The information in this book has been provided for educational & entertainment purposes only.

The information contained in this book has been compiled from sources deemed reliable, and it is accurate to the best of the Author's knowledge; however, the Author cannot guarantee its accuracy and validity and cannot be held liable for any errors or omissions. Changes are periodically made to this book. You must consult your doctor or get professional medical advice before using any of the suggested remedies, techniques, or information in this book.

Upon using the information contained in this book, you agree to hold harmless the Author from and against any damages, costs, and expenses, including any legal fees potentially resulting from the application of any of the information provided by this guide. This disclaimer applies to any damages or injury caused by the use and application, whether directly or indirectly, of any advice or information presented, whether for breach of contract, tort, negligence, personal injury, criminal intent, or under any other cause of action.

You agree to accept all risks of using the information presented inside this book. You need to consult a professional medical practitioner in order to ensure you are both able and healthy enough to participate in this program.

Table Of Contents

Chapter 1: Grasping Money Basics with Confidence 1

Chapter 2: Start Making Dollars 9

Chapter 3: Plan a Smart Budget 37

Chapter 4: Know the Tricks to Invest Money 65

Chapter 5: Learn the Art of Saving Money 99

Chapter 6: There Are Numerous Procedures to Earn Cash on Line 104

Chapter 7: Stats for Selling Designs and Art Technique 125

Chapter 8: Stats For Create EBooks Approach 139

Chapter 9: Creating a Membership Website Method 157

Chapter 10: Drop Shipping Business Method 168

Chapter 1: Grasping Money Basics With Confidence

Whether you're beginning from scratch, saving your allowance to create a strong destiny, or looking for out how you may make your coins give you the consequences you need, this economic break will guide you via the statistics you want to get to the bottom of the primary thoughts of coins, so that you recognize what to do with it when you get your hands on some!

What Role Does Money Play in a Teen's Life?

If you're like many teenagers, you can't do not forget coins due to the fact you still stay at home and spend most of your time at college You don't want a bargain money, nor do you have got had been given a whole lot of a hazard to earn it! However, reading about cash as a teenager is essential due to the fact it can offer you with a revel in of independence. You can exit with friends and notice a movie or have dinner and not using a want to borrow coins from your mother and father.

When you earn coins from an allowance or detail-time job, you're mastering responsibility. You see that your time and effort are nicely properly well worth price, which permits you assign a one-of-a-kind rate to cash than sincerely how masses it is able to buy you at a store.

As a excessive university pupil, you might not need coins for your schooling in case you're attending a public university with little to no prices, but at the same time as you graduate, you'll most likely have to pay for training. Whether you visit a network college, university, or alternate faculty or take a certification direction, you'll most probable need to pay for schooling, textbooks, and different fees. Scholarships and economic beneficial useful aid can help, but you'll want to cover some elements your self.

Learning about cash now, at the same time as it is able to now not make or damage you, offers you the chance to understand how a terrific deal you'll need in your lifestyles, for what capabilities, and the manner you may make investments and shop to set your self up for achievement inside the destiny.

Do All Teens Understand the Value of Money?

Everyone is specific, so it's comprehensible that you can now not recognize the fee of coins. It's a few problem that many have a look at handiest after they need to, which incorporates once they take on a detail-time interest or want to pay for his or her personal gasoline or car coverage. Once you start getting paid a positive quantity in your paintings or need to fork over your hard-earned cash just to get from factor A to element B, you begin to understand the fee of cash in a present day manner.

Many kids don't reflect onconsideration on cash as they develop up. When you're younger, you're lucky enough to have dependable adults and caregivers supplying steady haven, meals, garb, and one-of-a-kind requirements for you. If you're definitely fortunate, you moreover may moreover get toys, books, and unique devices that aren't critical for a very good lifestyles, however truely make subjects extra exciting. However, understanding that the good pair of denims prices $50 is specific than taking into account them as costing five hours of exertions at a short-meals restaurant! Therefore, the real rate of cash is some thing many teens don't look at until they get a venture.

When you earn your private money, you start to see matters in a one-of-a-kind way. You understand which you make a brilliant sum of money constant with hour, so that you higher apprehend no longer best the cost of cash, but furthermore the rate of the goods you purchase.

For instance, if you make $15 an hour and want to shop for a $a hundred pair of shoes that everybody at faculty is wearing, you'll must art work at the least seven hours to present you the cash for them (probably extra, relying at the earnings tax). However, from enjoy that traits to your college die out after a month.

Is it truely well worth it in case you want to artwork such masses of hours over severa days to shop coins for shoes that received't be cool for extremely long? Maybe, or in all likelihood no longer. But you're considering it from a unique factor of view as compared to how you used to ask your mother and father again and again to buy you some thing that emerge as the current fashion.

Do Teens Grasp Needs vs. Wants?

The idea of your mother and father and guardians imparting requirements begs the query: Do you apprehend the difference amongst needs and wants? Sometimes it is able to be difficult to logically suppose the query thru. If every person to your school has new shoes and also you don't, you'll probable sense which consist of you need them to wholesome in and avoid being the butt of the comic tale for the subsequent week.

However, if you have already got a long lasting pair of footwear, then you definately actually definately don't really need some component new.

You can test the distinction among needs and wants as you begin to earn coins and purchase your personal topics.

For example, you may think you need a vehicle to get to school every day. However, whilst you add up the associated charges, like coverage, fuel, and renovation, you could realize that all you actually need is transportation. A bus pass for some bucks a month can be the better deal than your very very own wheels.

With that during mind, you could apprehend how there are extraordinary degrees of wants and needs. You need meals to live, however it doesn't need to be a meal out with friends on a Friday night time time. While going out may be a blast, you'll learn the way you may take that cash and spend it on the grocery keep, getting enough meals to final you for each week! Taking a deeper take a look at what's within the again of your want and desires assist you to see matters in new approaches.

What Are the Essential Financial Terms a Teen Must Know?

There are many key financial terms you want to understand. This book will dive deeper into those ideas, however having a short evaluation will let you apprehend what to expect in future chapters.

Budget: A plan that factors for your earnings and costs that will help you control your coins. You'll tune wherein it comes from and how you spend it.

Compound interest: Compound interest is like earning hobby to your interest. When you shop or invest cash, you now not best earn hobby at the preliminary amount, however moreover at the interest that accumulates over time. This manner your coins can increase quicker, especially in case you start early and permit it compound over a few years.

Credit: The ability to borrow coins or get proper of entry to items and services without paying some component up the the front, however as an opportunity promising to pay it again later. Understanding how credit score score works is crucial to keep away from debt issues.

Credit rating: A range used by creditors to assess how probably you are to pay off loans, impacted by using manner of factors like credit score rating, debt, and if you've repaid loans inside the beyond.

Debt: Money you owe to someone else. You can increase debt from borrowing coins, and it usually comes with interest or charges.

Expenses: How you spend your cash, at the side of necessities like housing, meals, transportation, and special spending on gadgets like enjoyment and apparel.

Chapter 2: Start Making Dollars

You might imagine of coins as numbers on paper, however while you start making greenbacks, you'll have that paper on your hands and note it rework into stacks of cash! Learn the secrets and techniques in the again of being worthwhile thru allowance, babysitting gigs, and detail-time jobs you may juggle on pinnacle of your already entire time table. You may even harness your creativity and grow to be your very personal boss via launching an entrepreneurial mission. With the statistics on this financial ruin, you'll pass from having empty wallet to filling your piggy financial corporation with a lot coins that you need to deposit it on the economic group. In no time, you'll be looking that monetary organization stability develop!

Ways to Earn Money

Earning cash is manifestly a excellent step whether or not you desire to spend or maintain your fee range! But how will you get commenced out out? The outstanding difficulty is that there are numerous strategies to make cash these days. You can get a traditional manner, like running aspect-time for your community or babysitting inside the community. But you moreover may additionally additionally have clean get admission to to online opportunities, thanks to your telephone, pill, or laptop! More and greater younger people are also finding fulfillment as entrepreneurs, so information how you can tackle that mission will boom your earning capacity even more.

Traditional Jobs

There are many options for traditional jobs, which incorporates:

babysitting and domestic canine sitting

food company

garden care

lifeguarding

retail artwork

For positions in meals provider and retail shops, you could search for listings on line or visit the restaurants and shops to ask in the event that they're hiring. You'll maximum in all likelihood fill out an software and get an interview if they have an opening for you. Lifeguard roles are similar, despite the fact that your city authorities can also oversee community swimming pools and require a one-of-a-kind software program program system. Many businesses listing open positions on their web sites, so that you can look online to appearance in the event that they're hiring. You also can often fill out packages on line.

For babysitting, puppy sitting, and garden care, you could start on your network and work from there. You might also have pals with youngsters or pets, so speak to them about your company for once they need a date night or are taking place excursion. Establish yourself as honest and then encourage them to tell others about you so you e-book extra jobs. With those jobs and garden care, you can make a flier to cling at community stores, libraries, and community facilities. Include your touch statistics and services so human beings apprehend what to expect after they touch you.

Online Opportunities

You can promote your babysitting, doggy sitting, and garden care services on line manner to Facebook and nearby web sites like Nextdoor, but when you're at the internet, why no longer strong a far broader internet?

Freelancing is a notable way to make cash on line. Do you have got were given any of the following competencies?

photograph format

photographs

social media manipulate

net development

writing

If so, you may check out internet websites like Fiverr, Upwork, Freelancer, and one-of-a-kind paintings structures to connect with customers, deliver offerings, and gets a commission! With experience, you may even launch your very own net internet site and commercial enterprise—however you'll find out about that in the next phase.

You can paintings on-line finishing online surveys, as many organizations need human beings to conduct market research. Check out web sites like Survey Junkie and Swagbucks for possibilities.

While you may leverage your social media capabilities to manipulate commercial enterprise organization money owed, you can moreover spend time developing content on your very non-public shops. You can take pictures, record movies, write blogs, or file a podcast. You can earn coins with the useful resource of manner of monetizing your content fabric, both with the resource of net website hosting classified ads or having sponsors.

Good college students may additionally moreover need to teach to earn cash. You can display your buddies and classmates in man or woman, but while you offer your offerings online, you'll obtain a broader target marketplace. You can train college students wanting help with topics you've already taken, like decrease tiers of math and technological data, or find English language inexperienced individuals and help them draw close to grammar and conversational abilities.

Entrepreneurial Ventures

Becoming an entrepreneur includes some additives of the internet in this day and age, as noted above with net web hosting a podcast or YouTube channel, or starting a freelancing commercial enterprise. However, you could moreover promote gadgets as a company.

Drop-shipping and printing on call for are ways to sell products even as no longer having to pay up the the the front and keep physical items to your room. Use your design capabilities to offer art work clients might also want to make into shirts, notebooks, stickers, and greater on websites like Printify, Redbubble, Society6, and Zazzle.

If you're making devices like jewelry, fiber arts, and distinctive crafts thru using hand, you can start a shop on Etsy. It's one of the maximum famous web sites for homemade gadgets, so you could make correct cash with the aid of the use of listing your crafts there.

Not the entirety wishes to be on-line! You can begin a business enterprise for lawn care or vehicle washing and make fliers or use word of mouth for your neighborhood and city. You can also begin a commercial enterprise as an occasion planner, organizing events and gatherings for humans and companies. If you're a professional baker or prepare dinner, you may even sell desserts and selfmade treats or begin a small-scale catering enterprise.

Skills for Money-Making Success

Whether you work for a business organisation or begin your personal enterprise, there are positive competencies you need for coins-making success. Hard personnel understand their talents and recognize the significance of showing up and about their great. With cash-making talents, you'll stand out as an extremely good worker or industrial organisation owner, and this will empower you to artwork effectively and make more money in the technique.

Some key abilties consist of powerful communique, time manipulate, problem-solving, customer service, teamwork, and economic literacy. You most in all likelihood have already got factors of those talents based totally in your experience in university and with buddies. Transforming them that will help you at the mission can beautify your cash-making capability.

Communication Skills

Having appropriate communication talents is critical to succeeding to your each day life, but it's far specifically important at artwork. Here are some sensible guidelines that will help you decorate your communique capabilities:

Actively listen. This way you're showing others that you care approximately what they're saying.

Listen with out interruption. Summarize what they stated to make sure you understood it correctly. This abilities will assist you have got interplay with customers, colleagues, and your boss higher because of the truth you'll reduce down at the possibilities of misconception.

Be concise. This manner to mention or write subjects using as few phrases as feasible to get your element all through clearly and right away, without needless records or reasons.

The more concise you're with communication, the extra professional you'll stumble upon.

Hone your writing abilities. Read frequently and write each day, whether or not it's journaling, short reminiscences, or essays, to beautify your writing functionality.

Maintain eye touch and use exquisite frame language. Eye touch and open, excellent gestures show which you're engaged inside the verbal exchange.

Time Management

With particular time control, you'll have more time to make cash. However, you can experience which include you don't have the potential to cope with a few issue else. These recommendations will assist you control some time higher.

Prioritize responsibilities. Instead of dropping time procrastinating or doing a challenge you may outsource, use a while efficiently. Always begin with principal obligations as a way to make a large impact. Once you complete those, you'll experience greater green and note how an entire lot you can do with the aid of using taking motion.

Set dreams. This inspires you to be proactive. You can set each day or weekly dreams and mark them off as you complete them.

Divide obligations into viable steps. This permits you to preserve making progress in small quantities. You'll commonly have something to do to make development in the direction of the big photo, so that you don't waste time questioning what to do subsequent.

Manage it sluggish to stay stimulated. This can be difficult when you have hundreds on your plate. You'll want the pride of marking subjects off your to-do list, so chipping away at the task will assist you make development with out feeling beaten.

Remove distractions. Try to lower distractions like social media whilst analyzing or operating.

Learn to say no. Try not to overcommit. Be aware about your limits and set barriers to avoid overcommitting and feeling overwhelmed.

Take breaks. You may also count on you have to push thru a challenge until it's achieved, but it's higher to provide your thoughts and body a destroy. Walk spherical, get a few clean air, and do some thing else for a few minutes in advance than getting lower back to art work.

Problem-Solving Abilities

Along with communication abilities and time manipulate, honing trouble-solving abilties will make you a first rate asset to any art work group. It permits you figure out answers to troubles, like puzzles in a video game, and it makes you more impartial and assured. So, at the same time as you face tough situations, you'll be capable of discover your manner via and pop out more potent. Here are useful suggestions:

Analyze situations. Looking the least bit sides of an hassle can save you you from getting stuck in a trouble. You can speedy verify what occurred and brainstorm what to do to get out of it or restore it earlier than it becomes a larger trouble.

Practice often. Solve puzzles, riddles, and brainteasers often to exercise your hassle-solving muscle groups.

Think creatively. Encourage revolutionary wondering by brainstorming a couple of answers to a problem, despite the fact that they seem unconventional.

Be bendy and adaptable. You ought to be open to trade and inclined to go together with the drift,m so you don't experience caught and experience a problem while some thing adjustments within the 2d.

Learn from errors. Embrace mistakes as reading possibilities. Analyze what went incorrect and the way you may technique the trouble in some other manner subsequent time.

Be inventive. This characteristic allows you use your intelligence and what you have already were given to overcome any impediment that stands in your way. It goes with flexibility and modern questioning due to the truth you're actively finding a solution based totally on what's round you.

Collaborate with others. Work on company obligations or talk troubles with buddies and circle of relatives to benefit one of a kind views and mind.

Stay affected character. Problem-solving can take time, so be affected character and persistent. Don't get discouraged if a solution doesn't come without delay; maintain trying distinct techniques.

Customer Service

Customer provider is a talent that may take time to expand. When you're running in food provider or retail, you may have clients worrying subjects and treating you want you're an awful lot less than them. Read on for a few useful recommendations on dealing with clients.

Listen first. You may also have a line you deliver to all customers in positive situations, but while you take note of the customers to understand what they want, you can then communicate to them, actually so that they comprehend you're going to help them.

Handle clients well. This is a capacity that your supervisor and coworkers will word. When you draw close this knowledge, your boss will appreciate the manner you speak to clients and supply them what they need so that they come to be repeat internet page site traffic to the industrial organisation. You may additionally moreover even get rewarded with an advantage or boom!

Maintain a pleasant mind-set. Try to live calm, affected man or woman, and powerful, even in difficult situations. A great attitude can bypass an extended manner in making clients feel valued and respected.

Utilize hassle-solving abilities. You need to apprehend the client's trouble and characteristic a brief, powerful way to remedy it, so they revel in favored. You don't want to lose their agency, so think appreciably about what they want and the way you can make them happy.

Be empathetic. Even if a patron is being rude, you must exercise empathy and energetic paying attention to understand in which they're coming from. It's beneficial to region yourself in the purchaser's footwear to better deal with their problems.

Teamwork

Teamwork takes customer support a step beyond, regarding collaboration, assisting palms, and duty. The following hints will help you work with others.

Respect versions. You'll artwork with many people, from coworkers to teammates in sports activities sports to classmates you partner with for a faculty assignment. Embrace range inside your group. People have awesome backgrounds, opinions, and views. Respect those variations and use them for your gain.

Use exclusive competencies, along with problem-solving, lively listening, manual, and motivation. You may additionally need to juggle your obligations while supporting a person entire their paintings, which requires time manipulate and collaboration.

Create a joint mission. Say you need to begin a babysitting or garden care business agency, however apprehend you may't cope with all of the customers by myself. When you figure with a group of pals, you can serve more human beings and make extra money.

Pool assets. You may also want to start a images business business enterprise, however you first-rate have a virtual digicam. Working with someone who has image layout abilities will let you set up a net internet site, and you could provide each services to bring in greater clients.

Network. While you may pick out out to artwork on my own, teamwork will growth your risk of networking with folks who allow you to later. You might also need to make precious connections primarily based completely totally on who you recognise, which can result in better jobs—and coins-making opportunities—inside the future.

Financial Literacy

Financial literacy is the information you need to make the fine options alongside your coins. Below are tips that will help you addressing your cash.

Develop economic literacy facts. Financial literacy approach you apprehend how cash works and might manage it wisely.

Create a budget. Once you have got a price range, keep on with it! You should tune your fees and earnings.

Invest your coins. Financial literacy will assist you apprehend investment possibilities so you can broaden your wealth without installing extra time and effort than critical.

Avoid horrible debt. Not all debt is bad, but your facts will keep yours from spiraling out of manage and becoming now not viable to repay. You'll understand what debt you have to cope with.

Pay off the cash you owe. If you operate a credit score card, don't spend extra each month than you may pay decrease again without draining your financial organization account. Having an excessive amount of splendid debt manner you'll pay extra in hobby. If you can't pay it over again in a properly timed manner, you may damage your credit score score.

Benefits of Earning Money for Teens

The largest benefit of making a residing is which you have extra money to spend, proper? Well, type of. It's continuously a laugh to have the capacity to buy a elaborate coffee while you're out or get some component from the mall which you've been looking for weeks. With that in mind, you understand how having your non-public coins is essential for hundreds motives. However, you have to also store a few, and likely make investments it, to ensure you preserve having your very personal coins in preference to spending every paycheck as fast as you get it. When you check out those benefits of being worthwhile, you'll have a more understanding of the price it provides to your life.

Gives Financial Independence

Striving for more monetary independence as a youngster puts you in a terrific location to keep incomes your very non-public coins as an character. It can be tough to earn and keep cash, so whilst you begin now, you're developing super conduct to be able to serve you later. You can pay for your self on the same time as you go out with pals, not wanting to invite your mother and father to loan you coins for dinner or a movie. That offers you greater electricity over the way you spend your profits, because of the reality you won't need to provide genuinely each person a motive why you want to borrow coins.

When you're financially impartial, you best want to answer to your self. So, ensure you're spending coins on property you really want or want. Take time to ask your self what you're looking for and why.

Is it some aspect you really want? It's smooth to mention yes to those gadgets. Is it some thing you want? Think notably approximately why you want it. Is it a today's clothing object that lets in you to go out of favor next season? Is it a few thing each person at college has and you truly need to in shape in?

Consider your answers and assume in case you'd be happier with the object or with the cash. Because in case you don't without a doubt need or want the object, you may maintain the cash as an opportunity. When you begin saving, you'll have a cushion within the monetary institution for even as you want coins for an emergency or discover some thing you want to shop for.

Security

Speaking of getting a cushion in the financial institution, incomes profits offers you protection. You recognize you're capable of do paintings and receives a charge for it, which makes you revel in assured and regular to your capabilities. You have coins on the same time as you want it and can begin saving or making an investment to construct even greater wealth. Put your cash in a financial savings account with a immoderate interest price so that you can earn passive earnings every month, however despite the fact that withdraw the coins whilst you want it. If you're effective you obtained't need coins for a high-quality time, you'll in all likelihood want to do not forget setting it in a certificates of deposit (CD) because it will earn loads greater interest. Some banks offer CDs with a three-month shielding length, however you may make investments it for as a great deal as five years. When you withdraw the cash from the CD, you'll have manner more than you install—without doing something!

Earning your personal coins reduces financial pressure due to the truth you don't need to fear approximately borrowing from human beings. You'll have a protection net of cash, plus the potential to maintain earning extra through your art work. Instead of stressing approximately filling your vehicle with gas or getting rid of loans for college, you'll experience peace of mind know-how you're earning your personal cash to pay your way in lifestyles.

Skill Development

Working a detail-time activity permits you enlarge abilties as a way to serve you nicely later in life. Even in case you expect you're doing an average venture of ringing up clients at a fast-food area, you're still walking and growing capabilities. You're the usage of a cash join up, interacting with the general public, taking walks collectively with others, and showing up for shifts. No rely what pastime you have got got, even if you simplest artwork somewhere one afternoon in step with week, you'll be developing competencies you may later leverage to get higher—and better paying—jobs.

Rewind to when you acquire your first undertaking and bear in mind the competencies that the manner required. The act of utilizing for and getting a undertaking is already a valuable capability to have that you'll use hundreds on your life, and turning into shifts into your schedule and being punctual are key time manage abilties you want for success in all areas of your existence.

If you begin an entrepreneurial assignment, you'll increase even extra skills than even as you artwork for a person else. As the boss, you're going to discern out a manner to address a workload, make a product, address customers, and way the profits. In all jobs, you'll find out about teamwork, conversation, and trouble-fixing. You may not sense including you're growing abilities while you do a mission you're already familiar with, but you're reading extra than you recognize.

Planning for the Future

Earning cash now allows you intend for the destiny. Even in case you don't earn a lot at your element-time technique and ought to positioned that money towards fuel or vehicle coverage, you're already studying financial expertise a excellent way to serve you properly as you expand up. You get the danger to appearance how tough you discern and what form of coins you earn in your attempt. Then you pay for things you need or want and, with a chunk of good fortune, placed a few apart for the future. Even saving a small part of your income every month should make a huge distinction in phrases of your future financial savings capacity!

You'll boom forward-wondering as you earn cash. You understand how loads paintings you needed to do to earn a sure sum of money, so that you'll look ahead and recollect the manner you need to spend that money with out feeling consisting of you're throwing it away. You'll apprehend the significance of first-rate searching for property you really need or need and begin saving for university, making an funding, moving out, a automobile, and other large-price ticket gadgets.

Boosts Self-Confidence

Making your personal coins makes you feel unique! You're empowered to offer for your self, even if you don't need to but. When you may go out and purchase your own meals, espresso, treats, or amusing things, you feel proper about yourself. And when you have to put that cash toward bills, you revel in even higher due to the truth you understand you're growing a incredible life for your self. You can both contribute for your family and make your dad and mom a good deal a good deal much less confused about cash or pay in your personal fuel, automobile insurance, and distinct devices your parents also can cope with for you, regardless of the reality that they shouldn't must. Paying for yourself now will make you experience more potent approximately living independently and definitely paying your way in life.

Having a manner or on foot a industrial enterprise allows you recognize how you could make a dwelling inside the destiny. You're already reading what you like to do and what you're accurate at, so you recognize the way to leverage the ones skills to make cash. You're jogging with others to do a first-rate hobby and produce domestic a paycheck, so you'll enjoy assured in your talents and your functionality to get one-of-a-kind jobs inside the future. Having a manner to do and cash in the bank will make you enjoy like a assured character.

Activity

Do you recognize and appreciate the competencies you have got were given have been given and the manner they may can help you earn money? Answer these inquiries to location your self to the take a look at!

1. What hobbies or pastimes do you have? Think of 5 jobs which can make use of those abilities, whether it's jobs you'd look at for or approaches you could harness your entrepreneurial spirit and start your very very very own business.

2. What are five procedures you decided approximately in which you could artwork on-line to earn cash? Are any of these techniques ways you may use to boom your incomes functionality?

Chapter 3: Plan A Smart Budget

You've positioned a way to make coins, whether or not or now not you're babysitting or doing responsibilities across the town, working a retail mission, or walking your very very own industrial corporation. So… what now? Once you have got an profits, you want to installation a price range. This tool will help you tune how lots cash you are making each month in addition to the way you're spending it. Your budget can encompass many lessons for costs, alongside side critical payments, fun coins, and a difficult and fast amount to install your savings account or make investments for destiny financial safety.

Explore the Five Ws of Budgeting

Before you soar into budgeting, discover the 5 Ws to get history statistics. These questions will help you apprehend budgeting and the manner you may get the maximum out of this approach. It's not approximately being strict and stopping yourself from shopping for matters that make your existence higher.

Budgeting will become a mind-set that gadgets you up for financial achievement well into maturity, so it's excellent to start now.

Understanding the "Who" in Budgeting

You need to look at budgeting skills to serve you all through your existence. The more financially accountable you are, the more empowered you're to make cash and feature an emergency fund at the same time as no matter the fact that making ends meet. When you can manage your cash, you deliver your self independence. You won't ought to scramble to find out change within the couch cushions to shop for a coffee at the same time as you exit after university. You'll empower yourself to buy a automobile and lease an rental whilst you're equipped while not having to live home longer than you need or having to ask for help.

Basically, budgeting prepares you for maturity. It facilitates you are taking responsibility on your cash so you understand wherein it's far going and might keep consequently. Ideally, budgeting facilitates you keep away from debt. Even if you have a credit score card with a excessive restrict, higher than to spend greater than you can have enough cash, so that you don't need to borrow money or build up debt that can be difficult to pay lower again.

The sort of economic awareness you enlarge from budgeting will beautify your monetary self notion. You'll have a amazing deal a great deal less anxiety about cash due to the fact the way to allocate your price range to get what you need. You hone preference-making talents that help you determine out if you can purchase a few component or maintain the coins alternatively. These change-offs permit you to build your monetary economic financial savings due to the fact you think critically earlier than spending.

Remember that your budget is your commercial enterprise. You don't need to percentage information approximately your income and costs with everybody if you don't want to or don't be given as real with them. Your charge range and cash dreams are non-public, so don't allow certainly every person deter you from reaching your financial dreams.

Defining the "What" in Your Budget

If you believe you studied keeping a budget appears uninteresting or stifling, you'll love know-how there are many one-of-a-kind strategies.

Static budgeting: This is what you typically don't forget almost about budgeting. You create a hard and fast price range for the year primarily based absolutely to your predicted profits and prices. This gives you a clear outlook for the yr, but it isn't too flexible—or thrilling.

Flexible budgeting: This style is right for young adults due to the fact you can resultseasily adapt it in your desires. Your finances indicates your real lifestyles by manner of way of getting a bigger enjoyment price variety subsequently of the summer time months and more economic financial savings all through the winter on the identical time as you exit plenty much less with pals. However, the drawback is that it takes extra work to manipulate due to the fact you need to live on top of your spending and track the whole lot.

Envelope budgeting: This is each different high-quality technique for young adults as it's fingers-on. When you receives a commission, take out coins. Yes, having a economic financial savings account is exquisite, but for this technique, you need all of your coins on your palms. Label envelopes for each fee, along with financial savings, restaurants, entertainment, gas, and garb. Put a portion of your paycheck or stylish cash into each envelope ordinary with what you're probably to spend. Once you use all the coins in that envelope, you can't spend more in that elegance until your next paycheck. This technique keeps you responsible and permits you be conscious (literally) wherein your cash goes.

If any of the cited techniques above sound exciting, you can apply it to your every day lifestyles. However, you can also discover first rate techniques, or perhaps create one which works for you. To test out your budgeting fashion, start by means of using way of assessing your monetary dreams—each lengthy-term and brief-time period. You'll want to function instructions for what you want to save, so you'll have that included.

Take an honest check your income and costs. If you don't make a whole lot coins due to the fact you work issue-time, it's unrealistic to devise to excursion the region inside the subsequent months because of the reality you can't set aside enough financial financial savings. But this honesty lets in, due to the reality you'll see your dreams and try to fulfill them, so it's much less complex to reduce down needless spending.

You can constantly start with one budgeting approach and word the manner it works for you. If you find out which you're not saving sufficient and preserve pulling cash from particular categories, re-test your technique. Ensure you're breaking your dreams into capability steps and giving your self sufficient time to gain them.

For instance, you may begin saving for that revel in spherical the arena now and intention to make it a fact internal years. Having that remaining date have to make you experience extra practical with budgeting.

Timing Matters: "When" to Create and Review Your Budget

Finances change and you will possibly discover new wants to reap. You may possibly have sudden fees or get a car as a gift and need to vicinity money apart for gas and coverage. Your lifestyles isn't static, so your budget shouldn't be consistent each.

The greater you look at your price range, the greater you're thinking about your monetary state of affairs, which can decorate your economic savings capacity. Maybe you have a take a look at your charge variety after two months and comprehend you haven't spent any cash at eating places, so that you can put that into monetary financial savings and exchange the magnificence going beforehand.

Reviewing your price variety will display your spending styles and assist you've got a have a look at your need and goals. Maybe you've saved receipts that show you're spending too much money on apparel.

Think approximately how often and why you purchase garments. Do you placed on them sufficient to make it virtually worth the value? Try to lessen your clothing price range for a month or and look at how it affects you.

Regular finances opinions will help you adapt to changes on your existence and save you overspending, that may in reality throw you off route to your prolonged-term dreams.

Allocating Resources: "Where" Your Money Goes

The biggest attraction of a rate range is being capable of see in which your money is going. If you discover yourself brief on payments or pulling from monetary financial savings each month, you'll understand that you need to test your price range and make some modifications.

Start thru reviewing the necessities, at the side of payments and fees, which may be critical in your every day lifestyles. For now, those necessities would probably only include your cellular cellphone bill, vehicle coverage, and gasoline, but analyzing the manner to allocate your cash now will help you inside the future on the equal time as your requirements consist of housing, groceries, utilities, and healthcare. Write down your recurring month-to-month charges to look wherein that money goes. Then, you may take steps to lessen corners indoors the ones categories, like finding a greater tons less high priced mobile cellphone provider or being extra efficient together with your errands so you use a whole lot much less fuel.

You have to additionally allocate coins for monetary financial savings. Ensuring you could positioned cash away every month will offer you with a buffer whilst you hit surprising expenses. You can pull cash out of your emergency fund in case you're short on earnings one month. You also can save coins within the route of quick-time period dreams, like shopping for a new pc or scoring concert tickets.

Your spending can even embody a discretionary fund, that's fun cash. This is a few different place in which you may lessen corners in case you're now not capable of pay your super payments. Discretionary rate variety can encompass coins you spend on films, restaurants, video video games, pursuits, shopping for, and journey. Write down in which the whole lot is going so that you can understand your spending behavior.

Discovering the "Why" Behind Your Budget

A smart budget manner you're prioritizing your monetary stability at the same time as nevertheless shopping for the belongings you need with out being wasteful. You can create a clever rate range thru setting desires, like shopping university, looking for a car, or happening holiday. When you've got a reason in thoughts, you may create an in depth technique to how you'll keep that money.

Include all earnings, like paychecks from a task and allowance out of your mother and father. Then, write down everything you spend on every month, whether or now not or not it's for school lunches, nights out with friends, fuel for your automobile, or specific fees. When you stay independently, those charges will consist of your lease, groceries, utilities, and exceptional huge payments.

Always embody region for economic financial savings, however be practical. You need a smart price range, not a few trouble impossible that makes you experience awful even as you fall quick.

For example, don't say you're going to shop $ hundred a month while you top notch make $3 hundred from your aspect-time mission and want to pay for gasoline, nights out with pals, or new clothes.

Prioritize saving coins and only spending what you need to spend, but also be bendy with yourself. Know that some months you can encounter sudden expenses and be no longer capable of hold in any respect, and surely roll with it even as that occurs. You'll already have the clever fee range mind-set, so that you can live in this financial financial savings route with out feeling like you've out of place your goal.

Strategies to Plan a Smart Budget

Planning a smart budget takes paintings. Even when you have an notable idea of the way plenty coins you're making in comparison to what you spend, putting it on paper (or in an app!) may help you be aware subjects otherwise. Money may be precis for some human beings, in particular if your pastime will pay through direct deposit and you spend coins with a debit or credit card. When you don't preserve the cash and phrase it leaving your hands, it's greater hard to comprehend how lots you're really making and spending.

Check Your Earnings

Before you can budget your cash, you need to understand how tons you have got got coming in. Your profits include any income you're making on a semi-ordinary foundation, so that you can difficulty it into your fee variety.

For instance, if you artwork at a shop within the mall after college and babysit every weekend, you may calculate the ones earnings into your budget. However, if you handiest earn cash while you mow the grass at home, you'll have a more difficult time establishing a fee variety you may maintain on with, because you acquired't have a difficult and rapid mowing schedule inside the course of the yr.

Therefore, the information in the previous chapter approximately finding a pastime is essential! You want to find a few detail that offers a everyday paycheck, with out taxing yourself an excessive amount of in phrases of juggling college and your different obligations.

Even if you have a undertaking, your hours may also variety week with the useful resource of week. You may additionally need to take day off for a college event or excursion to a competition with the band or a set. When you don't work a hard and speedy time desk, your pay can variety every month. However, you can though estimate your income for budgeting competencies, and fill in the actual quantities when you get your paychecks for the month.

Plan Your Essential Expenses

The key to a pleasant budget is to pay all your critical prices first. If you need to pay for fuel and vehicle insurance, the ones come out of your earnings in advance than some thing else. If you live independently, you need to prioritize lease, coverage, utilities, and groceries considerably. Essential fees are ones you'd maximum probably have every month. Even in case you pay automobile coverage each six months, you can add it into your monthly fee range to ensure you have got the money even as you want it.

One exceptional manner to recognize budgeting is the "50-30-20" rule. This approach you spend 50% of your earnings on assets you want, 30% on things you need, and 20% on savings. How you spoil down that 30% for dreams is as masses as you. Let's test out an instance.

If you're making $1,000 a month, due to this $500 goes closer to your fees, like food, automobile insurance, fuel, and college needs. You can spend $three hundred on a few component you need, which might also imply you allocate $a hundred for going out with pals, $a hundred for video games, and $one hundred for fast food. Maybe you want to spend $one hundred fifty for date nights, $50 on gourmand espresso, and $one hundred on decor on your room. This elegance is the only that has the maximum flexibility, due to the fact you understand that $500 is for dreams and $ hundred is for financial savings.

Define Your Expenditure Limits

Your limits need to fall inner how lots cash you earn, of route, but past that, you have were given plenty of flexibility with every class you create. Once you placed aside cash in your important prices, you can choose categories collectively with:

clothing and add-ons

enjoyment with buddies

video video games, music, and films

eating places

economic economic financial savings

You also can create more famous classifications, like "desires" and "economic monetary savings." You can located a part of your profits into financial financial savings and then spend the rest however you be aware healthful, whether or not or no longer or now not it's searching for the ultra-present day video game or going to a pizza location alongside facet your buddies every Friday. Even despite the fact that you're not budgeting for each object, you're even though sticking to a enormous spending limit to help you hold cash.

Set Your Saving Goals

While your charge variety will assist you be aware where you spend cash, you need to additionally set some aside for monetary financial savings. Start by manner of manner of figuring out a motive for your financial monetary savings account. It can be a concrete purpose, like having $1,000 with the useful resource of the give up of the year or having a down price for a vehicle earlier than your next birthday. It also can be greater summary, like just seeking to shop coins so that you'll have a safety net if you want it. You can even installation financial financial savings money owed for exceptional functions, like a stylish monetary savings account and some other for your cause.

Track your financial savings to your price variety sincerely as you song expenses. You want to look how lots you positioned aside each month, whether or not it's usually $50 or a percentage of your earnings that might range over time.

Allot Money for Emergency Funds

Regardless of your precise savings dreams, an emergency fund is a smart preference. When you add this object in your price variety, you're ensuring your self a protection net in case a few component unexpected happens. Maybe you need to buy precise substances for a college mission on the remaining minute or want to pay for vehicle maintenance. Knowing which you have coins set aside for that type of prevalence can alleviate masses of strain. This account is one you could preserve adding to and permit the hobby rate add extra cash monthly so that you constantly have rate variety reachable, regardless of what your month-to-month finances also can appear to be.

Use Budgeting Apps

Keeping a paper budget is probably uninteresting. Maybe you're not a spreadsheet individual, both. Thankfully there are budgeting apps which can be clean to use. Best of all, they're available! You can tune your spending on the equal time as you're on the pass, in region of forgetting what you bought by the time you're making it home after a long day. Look into the ones apps to look how they could help:

Expensify

Goodbudget

Mint

PocketGuard

You Need a Budget (YNAB)

As an energetic teen, you have were given already got loads taking place for your lifestyles. Budgeting could probably appear like every unique venture you have to discover time for, so that you positioned it off. However, economic safety is so essential which you actually should prioritize budgeting. Therefore, linking a budgeting app in your bank account and credit card will right away tune records with out you having to do any of the paintings your self.

Leave Scope for Adjustments

Even with a thoughtful price range, you're but going to have a few changes each month. Perhaps you needed to address an surprising car repair earlier than you had enough cash to your emergency fund to cowl it. Or you had to buy birthday or tour offers for your loved one and forgot to feature it to the price range.

Being capable of adjust your budget every month will empower you to take even greater manage over your costs and economic financial savings. Instead of blindly following the identical recommendations, you're actively assessing your price range and changing it while vital.

Plan Your Budget Every Month

Some human beings make annual budgets to make certain they live on course for lengthy-term desires, but it's best if you plan your fee variety every month. This gets you in the dependancy of considering your cash more regularly than at the start and give up of the 12 months. When you are making a monthly fee variety, you could check your schedule and plan therefore. Maybe you need to buy a birthday present in your exquisite friend or charge range coins for a date night time. You may additionally need to vicinity extra into economic financial savings due to the fact you don't have extra fees this month and need to cushion your emergency fund.

Planning your rate range every month additionally gives you a danger to appearance lower lower returned over your spending. You can see what you spent and saved closing month to get a higher statistics of your behavior. Regularly checking on this type of statistics let you adapt your attitude for a more potent monetary technique shifting beforehand.

Benefits of Budgeting for Teens

Budgeting is crucial because it helps you control your coins, even in case you don't have a whole lot. The act of creating a budget calls for crucial thinking, and sticking to it's far even greater fantastic! Making and keeping a fee variety can reduce the strain and tension you revel in in terms of looking to pay for your non-public topics or shop up for massive purchases, so it's a extremely good talent to exercise as you end up older.

Helps Manage Finances

When you have were given a budget, you can see how an awful lot cash you convey in and wherein it's miles going. Whether you have got a venture, get an allowance, or get coins as gadgets, your income is vital and you want to spend efficiently. Making a rate range beforehand of time allows you see how a incredible deal coins you want every month in your bills or amusing outings with buddies. Checking over your prices on the cease of each month will show you what you clearly spent and in which that money went.

For instance, if you end up spending extra on meals out with buddies, you could decide to boom that rate range elegance the following month. If you need to shop more, you may get stricter with your self even as you exit. You wouldn't have any of this records with out a charge range, even though, so it genuinely permits manipulate price variety.

Makes Scope for Savings

If you get cash and spend it in advance than it even hits your wallet, you're not able to maintain some thing. Creating a rate range offers you a chance to take a look at your earnings and prices and tell your self how an awful lot you could spend on each category, in conjunction with putting cash into financial economic financial savings.

A economic monetary savings account is essential due to the fact you will in all likelihood need to keep up for some thing big, like a car or your first rental. You may also additionally want to preserve cash for university lessons. You and your friends can also moreover plan to take fun journeys or visit stay performance activities, and your financial savings account can cover the ones charges. Even in case you don't have something in mind to maintain up for, developing an emergency account will give you financial safety in the future.

Reduces Money-Related Stress

That emergency fund will reduce cash-associated pressure, but so does budgeting in stylish. When you track how an lousy lot coins you are making and spend, you received't experience annoying questioning when you have sufficient to cowl certain bills or fun activities each month. You'll have already calculated a price variety that gives you coins for each vital rate in your existence.

You might not be rolling in dough, however budgeting some thing coins you have got got can reduce pressure due to the fact you still be without a doubt on pinnacle of factors. You comprehend exactly how a super deal cash you have got got and can inform your self what to spend it on and what kind of to save, which gives you a experience of power over your life if you want to reduce stress and anxiety.

Establishes Good Money Habits

Budgeting places you within the mind-set of creating and following right cash conduct. When you start budgeting the cash you're making from an allowance or detail-time challenge, you're schooling yourself how to take care of your needs financially. This ability will serve you nicely as you expand up and function you to come to be an grownup who's on pinnacle of factors in their coins and may live a financially snug life.

You're already learning the manner to consider every greenback you earn, spending it carefully on assets you want and need. You'll moreover apprehend the significance of monitoring your spending, which serves you properly whilst you open a credit score card. You'll already recognize how to test your expenses, so that you're plenty much less likely to get a wonder credit score score rating card invoice with a massive great stability.

Budgeting is a expertise you'll increase over time, so beginning now empowers you to store cash and spend thoughtfully. It includes monitoring your profits and fees, so that you normally recognise how a lot cash you bring in and the manner you're spending it. This exercising enables you are making thoughtful spending picks and teaches you the way to prioritize monetary financial savings. Over time, you'll boom monetary region and obligation, putting you up for success as you reach maturity and produce in a larger earnings.

Activity

Before you create a rate range, you want to music your costs. Save your receipts for three months or song your spending thru your on line economic organisation account or credit score rating card announcement to fill out this worksheet. Three months will offer you with a threat to notice a sample on your spending. It moreover offers you a few leeway, like if you spend masses in December because you're looking for items for others, however don't spend as a good buy in November and January.

There are recommendations stuffed in on the issue of area to jot down down all the manner all the way down to your distinct purchases.

Be sincere with yourself proper right right here, as this could assist you price range. You may additionally examine that you spend lots of cash looking for random tech, like earbuds or webcams. You would possibly visit a store and buy make-up or random items just to have some thing to do. Write down every charge so that you may also want to make a sensible price range for your self.

Once you fill within the worksheet, highlight the call of the important costs. Look at how plenty you spent during the last 3 months and spot if there's a sample. Maybe you spend $one hundred a month on coffee that would be stored by using manner of way of brewing cups at domestic. Maybe you exit to eat with friends even in case you've already had dinner at home, definitely to be social, but you emerge as shopping for a meal you don't eat. Make notes on what you're spending and assume severely about why you spend this cash.

Chapter 4: Know The Tricks To Invest Money

You might imagine you're too young to start making an funding cash, but the earlier you begin, the more you boom your earning capability. When it includes investments, you may choose immoderate- or low-chance options. With excessive-risk investments, you may in all likelihood make a whole lot of coins right away, but you can moreover lose coins. For low-risk investments, you can make investments coins now and leave it for over 30 years or until retirement, giving it time to develop slowly but really. However, earlier than you begin investing, you want to apprehend the fundamentals.

You can invest in shares, bonds, mutual finances, CDs, or maybe actual belongings. Each preference has experts and cons that allow you to defend and develop your coins. When you do not forget each of these options, you want to consider your desires. Are you looking to store a number of cash in just a few years to pay your college classes?

Do you want to shop for a residence by the point you turn 30, giving your cash 12 to 15 years to grow? Or are you saving for retirement and might effortlessly located cash away for 50 years to create a massive nest egg to live off within the future? Goals impact the shape of investment you have to select out out, so study at once to analyze what you need to recognize to make your cash be honestly proper for you.

What Is Investing?

Investing sounds intimidating to many people because of the reality your coins can also moreover seem locked away. If you invest in real belongings or a CD, you can't dip into them on the equal time as you need a hint extra money like you could withdraw out of your savings account. But you want to moreover maintain in thoughts that, at the same time as invested properly, your coins has superb capacity to broaden. While you may't with out trouble get proper of get entry to to it, you're going to have a larger nest egg the longer you allow it take a seat down, so it's really well worth having staying energy to gain economic success.

The Power of Compound Interest

Compound interest seems like magic because of the reality your coins grows without you looking to perform a little component in any respect. When you picture yourself being profitable, you likely see your self at work, earning $15 or so in keeping with hour. After hours, your coins is now $30; after a 4-hour shift, you have got $60. Your cash is developing, but you're running hard for it. With compound hobby, you don't need to do the artwork.

Let's say you make investments $100 in a economic organization account that has an annual hobby rate of five%. At the surrender of the primary year, you'll earn 5% of $100, bringing your account overall as tons as $100 and five. That way, going into the second yr of the account, it's together with you've invested $one hundred and five, and the five% interest is on top of that amount in place of your initial funding. So, via manner of way of the quit of the second one 365 days, you'll have earned $five.25 in hobby, bringing your new economic organization balance as a great deal as $a hundred and ten.25. In years, you'll have made $10.25 with out doing some thing.

That quantity may also seem small, but consider that some debts have particular hobby charges, and the extra you make investments, the more you'll make. Compound interest want to encourage you to region extra cash in the path of monetary financial savings in place of spending it on coffee and food out with pals, due to the reality you'll preserve earning increasingly.

Why Should Teens Start Investing Early?

You should begin making an investment early because it's an extended-time period recreation, so beginning now gives you even greater time to allow your cash increase. The market will truely have americaand downs, so the longer you may depart your cash on my own, the more likely you'll make more from the interest and investments. Retirement also can additionally appear a long manner away, however the years will fly by the usage of way of. As you're busy dwelling your brilliant existence, your investment bills can be developing to provide you with a financially stable destiny on your golden years.

Investing now enables you construct proper conduct due to the fact you're learning to hold and be smart along side your cash. You also can see making an investment as a mastering opportunity because of the truth you'll hold an eye available inside the market and learn the way it can rise and fall, and what issues make that display up! You'll start making informed alternatives based totally on important wondering and processing statistics from a couple of assets, targeted to your financial health.

By making an funding now, you're putting your self up for economic independence. You should make smart choices that make it clean for you to shop for a state-of-the-art automobile, pay your university schooling, or pass from your parent's home into your very very very own rental. Making the most of those life landmarks manner you need to have monetary records, and investments will let you get there.

Interesting Ways to Invest Money for Teens

Investing cash is a smart manner to end up financially regular. However, making an funding may appear silly and complicated. Once you check out all the unique options, you'll see that there are various interesting methods to make investments money and maximize your incomes capacity. Based to your goals and hobbies, you can decide to play it stable with a financial savings account or journey the roller coaster of the inventory market.

Stock Market

The stock market can also appear like it has the fine highs and the lowest lows, but that's truly what you pay attention approximately within the information. Starting in the stock marketplace is a high-quality way to invest your money and growth wealth. The inventory marketplace gives you the chance to shop for shares of possession in organizations. The businesses use the coins from promoting stock to pay for their business. If the company does wel , the value of the stock increases and you may sell it for extra than you initially paid.

The inventory marketplace is a outstanding manner to assemble wealth over time. If you could make investments money in a business enterprise and leave it, you're much more likely to earn cash because the employer grows. You should recognize approximately the risks and marketplace dispositions, despite the fact that, which means that that that you could now not make your cash again and must promote at a loss.

You can research stock exchanges similar to the New York Stock Exchange (NYSE) and Nasdaq. Companies list their shares on those stores so that you can buy shares thru a brokerage account. When you buy a share of stock, you currently have possession in that organization and might benefit from its income. The price of a inventory can change each day and with name for, so you want to investigate whilst to shop for a stock earlier than the fee goes up because of the reality truly absolutely everyone wishes it. Websites like Fidelity, Charles Schwab, and Ameritrade will will allow you to get started with research and making an funding.

If you're interested by making an funding within the stock market, but you're below 18, you may speak on your parents or guardians and open a custodial brokerage account. Together with the individual, you may at the same time manage the account till you're 18 and take entire manipulate.

Bonds and Fixed-Income Investments

Stocks are one of the maximum commonly appeared investments, however bonds and glued-earnings investments are also high-quality picks for young adults. Basically, bonds are loans you deliver to a business enterprise or the government. You buy a bond, giving them your cash to use as they see healthful. They promise to pay you back at a certain date, providing you with the authentic amount you paid plus hobby bills in the interim. The interest bills are a percentage of the bond's face rate.

Bonds aren't as unstable due to the fact the stock marketplace. Because you're loaning coins to a company or the authorities, you're guaranteed to get your cash lower back plus interest, so there's no need to anticipate the rise and fall of charge just like the inventory market. While you're prepared to gather the bond's maturity date, you'll get coupon bills of hobby, so you'll get passive income within the route of your wait.

You may think bonds appear dull in contrast to the interesting capacity of the stock market, however the awesome aspect is that you may spend money on each! Diversification essentially technique you're now not setting all your eggs in a unmarried basket. Instead of making an funding $1,000 in the inventory marketplace, you may invest $500 there and $500 in bonds, growing your incomes ability and providing you with extra possibilities to make investments. These payments make up your portfolio, that could be a fancy word which means the collection of your investments.

Mutual Funds

Mutual charge variety are investments that pool coins from many customers to shop for diverse belongings, which includes stocks and bonds, so that you have coins taking walks for you in considered one of a kind strategies. You don't want to actively track your investment as loads because of the reality a expert fund supervisor oversees matters, making the excellent funding selections for everybody involved. Since you buy stocks of the fund with others, you don't want to present as lots money to get many precise investment options.

Instead of looking to test numerous investment options, mutual budget are high-quality for teens because your cash will skip in the direction of many assets for the great diversification. It reduces the hazard of terrible-acting investments because of the fact you've got such a lot of energetic options. There's a expert manager, so that you can sit down again and allow your coins be just right for you whilst no longer having to show the stock marketplace and test the fee of your funding each day. Also, because you're pooling belongings with distinct shoppers, it's one of the maximum low value alternatives. If you need that money short, you can purchase or sell shares due to the fact your funding stays considerably liquid as compared to extraordinary options. You can also always invest more money in mutual finances to growth your investment payout.

Exchange-Traded Funds

Exchange-traded price range (ETFs) are investments within the inventory marketplace, however they're more diverse than purchasing for a single business enterprise's stock, so you can greatly boom your incomes capability. You can pick a specific institution, like bonds, commodities, or stocks, and notice economic growth from numerous resources.

For instance, you may put money into a inventory ETF that owns stock in lots of special agencies across industries.

Yes, you're making an funding in the stock marketplace best, but you're going to get plenty of options with that one funding, that could pay off. They're also decrease price in comparison to controlled mutual fee variety, so extra of your cash goes without delay to the stock instead of the manager.

Like mutual finances, ETFs provide liquidity, which means that that you may sell stocks at some degree within the shopping for and selling day in case you want to get proper of access to money. You don't ought to fear about your cash getting tied up inside the inventory and being no longer able to pay your payments. Even despite the fact that you've invested a certain amount in ETFs, you may sell stocks to get the coins in coins alternatively of getting to wait a hard and fast time frame to get proper of entry to it.

You can spend money on an ETF now by using starting an funding account; get assist from a mum or dad in case you're underneath 18. You can choose an ETF based totally to your economic goals and what kind of hazard you're inclined to take in conjunction with your coins. When you regularly make a contribution even small portions of money, you'll see a massive growth on your rate range.

Savings Accounts

Savings payments are the maximum steady funding opportunity due to the fact your cash stays within the economic institution, and the Federal Deposit Insurance Corporation (FDIC) insures your cash as plenty as a sure limit. This approach that the economic organization can run into hassle and you'll though have your full sum of money insured, so that you gained't skip broke simply due to the truth the financial group closes down. It's smooth to open a financial savings account at any financial institution near you, and you can withdraw coins every time you want it.

With that during mind, you can without problems open a savings account for emergency fee range, college training, a automobile, or any other purpose you have in mind. In maximum times, you'll need to have a central authority-issued ID and Social Security variety. If you're beneath 18, you'll want a decide or father or mother to cosign with you, clearly as you need them for other funding options.

A monetary savings account facilitates you earn money because of its hobby price. Some banks have low hobby prices, so store round for one so that it will pay off in time. You can deposit cash frequently and spot your savings increase because of the modest hobby rate.

If you want to beautify your economic literacy, starting with a economic monetary financial savings account as an funding opportunity is the high-quality manner to move. You'll discover approximately deposits, withdrawals, hobby, and financial savings. You can tune your account on-line or via an app so you can effects combine a monetary savings account into your budgeting technique.

Certificates of Deposit

CDs are particular financial financial financial savings payments banks provide, in order that they're furthermore insured via the FDIC. They have a specific time restrict and a higher interest price than a desired financial financial savings account. The entice is which you need to preserve your cash in the CD till the time is up, in any other case you'll need to pay a penalty.

For instance, you could located $500 in a CD for 365 days and get an interest price that can be double what the bank gives on popular economic financial savings payments. At the stop of the term, you could withdraw $750 or greater counting on the hobby rate, however you may't withdraw any cash before the surrender of the term.

CDs are accurate investment options for teens because of the fact they're secure and payout in a large way. There's no risk of dropping your funding like there may be with the stock market. You'll moreover take a look at plenty approximately interest via making an funding in CDs. You'll increase problem with the useful resource of being not capable of get entry to that investment, so it may really help you exchange your financial conduct.

Visit your economic group and ask what CDs they offer. You can pick out the terms primarily based on how a excellent deal cash you need to earn or how lengthy you may keep that money tied up. Once the CD time period ends, you may withdraw the cash with out final results. You also can decide to resume the CD and hold earning more money out of your initial funding.

Real Estate Investing

Real property making an investment may be tough for teens to break into because it requires a enormous up-the the front investment, but analyzing approximately it now will allow you to make appropriate choices in the future.

For example, you could have the goal of saving sufficient cash now to buy a residence close to campus by the point you join up in college. You can live there until commencement, then rent it out to first-rate college college students to make cash on the same time as you flow into some place else.

Real estate investments are whilst you buy belongings to generate profits. You can do this both with the aid of using buying a property, like a residence or rental to lease, or making an funding in actual belongings funding trusts (REITs). REITs are businesses that finance income-producing real estate, so you ought to make cash thru being part of their organisation.

Real assets is one of the excellent strategies to assemble lengthy-term wealth because most assets values boom through the years, and those continuously want an area to live, so you're basically assured capacity earnings with assets in a manner you're no longer with the stock marketplace. You can generate constant passive earnings by means of way of manner of renting out a assets.

As a teenager, you'll want to analyze REITs to get a taste of real belongings investments. You can understand the real property market at the same time as no longer having sufficient coins to buy a residence on your non-public. There are many varieties of REITs, which incorporates residential, enterprise, and retail, so that you can invest in unique assets classifications. Commercial real property consists of any assets used for industrial commercial enterprise organisation functions in location of dwelling areas. Retail real property consists of homes and homes for shops, purchasing facilities, and department shops. Generating earnings via an REIT permit you to develop wealth and make you excited to spend money on real assets more while you've earned sufficient coins.

There are plenty of techniques to make investments your cash, and all have benefits and risks. Consider your monetary dreams and what kind of you may make investments now in advance than creating a preference. Research is high and speak to your mother and father or guardians approximately what they're inclined to help you with almost about cosigning and custodial accounts, which provide you access to their debts and credit score playing playing cards so that you can discover ways to manage cash with plenty less chance for your credit score and rate range.

Factors to Consider for Teen Investors

Learning about the numerous funding possibilities is simply the end of the iceberg. You want to broaden your wealth, however you need to recognize exactly what you're entering into. There are risks concerned with any investment, so you need to consider how lots coins you're inclined to lose for the danger to earn greater than you can keep in mind. Being open with yourself about your alternatives will help you are making knowledgeable decisions concerning investments.

Risk Tolerance

Before you invest a penny, you need to consider your chance tolerance. When you invest $one hundred in the inventory market, you may watch it increase to $1,000 or see it dwindle away so that you lose coins in your investment. You want to don't forget how inclined you are to look your cash variety. It can be tough to appearance your hard-earned coins make numerous hundred dollars and then lose it involved approximately no motive you could apprehend. You also need to consider your capability to lose this cash. If you haven't any financial savings and want money to pay payments, it's higher you maintain your $a hundred in preference to creating an investment it, on account that you could possibly lose all of it.

Since you're making plans to start making an investment as a youngster, you can tackle more chance. You have many years earlier than you'll want a number of this cash within the case of retirement making an funding, so that you don't want to fear approximately dropping quite a few cash proper now due to the fact you received't need it till later. You may additionally want to even invest coins in severa stocks and debts which can be a combination of excessive and espresso chance, to make sure you have got investments prepared for the close to destiny and in your retirement.

Time Horizon

As you can apprehend from studying about danger tolerance, your timeline could make a large distinction to your investment approach. Since you're beginning extra youthful, you have greater time to allow money to increase at a slower tempo. The market fluctuations obtained't have an impact on you as a bargain due to the fact even a excessive loss however has time to develop and offer you with a awesome payout. Market fluctuations can appear based mostly on politics, the economic system, or certainly one of a type additives that effect every day lifestyles and the value of coins. That can suggest the price of your money owed changes significantly every day, however will also out over the years.

People who don't invest until they're older don't have that lots time. If a person is 50 and wants to create a retirement account, they'll exceptional have 15 years to get enough cash to live off of once they surrender art work. They'll want to tackle extra hazard via way of selecting shares that may supply extra feasible earnings in a shorter quantity of time. Since you've got were given 50 or extra years earlier than retirement, you may invest a extremely good deal much less coins in lower-threat bills and note extra of a payout than the 50-yr-vintage investor ever will.

However, you moreover may additionally want to don't forget it slow horizon in terms of each aim. Saving for retirement is one detail, but you may want to keep to pay college instructions in the following few years. You can also in fact need to begin a monetary financial savings account for an emergency fund of cash you may get right of access to at any time. Consider all factors of your desires and timelines to ensure you make investments carefully and may offer for a few element you want.

Diversification

Learning about all of the funding alternatives with a piece of properly fortune grabbed your interest. Even if simplest one investment opportunity sounded exciting, you have to undergo in mind diversification. In most instances, it'll pay off to have cash in a couple of investments due to the reality you'll continuously earn greater in assessment to retaining your coins in a low-hobby account.

When you diversify your investments, you unfold the threat of dropping your cash and tanking your incomes ability. If the stock market takes a nosedive, you may not lose all your coins because of the reality your bonds and ETFs can however hold consistent.

As a teenager, you want to find out all your options. Even if stocks seem to have the most functionality, you need to moreover try bonds, ETFs, and REITs. You're younger, so that you have time to make once more any money you may lose in an investment method that's no longer proper for you. However, you would possibly apprehend that a few aspect that seemed dull on the begin is actually a high payday. Try all your options in advance than identifying you need to live with one or two funding opportunities—you will be amazed at the very last consequences.

Research and Due Diligence

This phase might in all likelihood have made you excited to make passive earnings, this means that you can generate cash without operating, like through the stock marketplace and compound interest. Hopefully it moreover showed you the manner important it's far to investigate earlier than taking motion. You might imagine it's clean to create a brokerage account and start making an investment, but you want to recognize what you're getting into. Research shares, bonds, mutual price range, and other belongings earlier than you prevent a penny of your very private cash. You need to recognize what a employer does and the way probable they're to make a earnings. Even if you plan to offer a fund supervisor entire manipulate of your coins, you want to have a few fundamental records about what you're doing for danger evaluation, if not some thing else.

Check financial information net web sites and investment books for facts in this approach. You can also speak to your mother and father or depended on economic advisors to get custom designed advice on making an investment to your precise goals.

Investing as a teenager is a chief bounce ahead, not handiest putting you on the proper route in the direction of economic independence, however moreover imparting you with a leg up for wealth-constructing. When you are taking your foundational understanding and take into account hazard tolerance and your timeline, you're getting ready yourself to make knowledgeable picks to help you reap your economic desires.

Simple Steps to Start Investing for Teens

Learning approximately the types of funding opportunities offers you a giant assessment of methods you could get started out on this hassle. However, you want to take a deeper dive to ensure you recognize what steps you need to take to make investments your cash inside the smartest way feasible. By following those steps, you can start on your journey of monetary empowerment. Your investments will construct a sturdy basis for your destiny monetary success.

Step 1. Explore and Learn About Investing Options

The first step inside the direction of creating an investment is to discover, test, and conduct studies. This bankruptcy is a first-rate manner to get started out out getting to know, however it's in general huge information to characteristic your launchpad. You'll want to get more precise on your studies through looking deeper into stocks, bonds, mutual price variety, ETFs, REITs, and different investment possibilities. There are dangers and rewards associated with each opportunity, so that you'll need to take notes after which check which align best at the aspect of your financial goals and preferred method to cash.

While it's excellent to start making an investment as soon as you may, that absolutely refers to beginning now, at the same time as you're a youngster and function your complete life in advance of you. That doesn't endorse you need to bypass taking some weeks to investigate earlier than you give up your difficult-earned money. Look on line for property, books, and courses tailor-made in the course of youngster and amateur buyers. This data is probably more reachable because of the truth you gained't need notable economic facts, and may be greater approachable because it obtained't require which you have thousands of dollars ready to invest.

Step 2. Set Clear Investment Goals

Before handing over coins, you need to understand your funding goals and apprehend that your approach will help you achieve them.

For example, in case you're 16 and need to shop cash to pay for college, putting your issue-time paycheck in a monetary financial savings account received't assist you earn as plenty coins as you'll want in the close to destiny. With that goal and timeline, it's better to examine a CD with a excessive interest fee and make investments your cash for 2 years to peer it develop.

You might not have a set intention for your investment. People saving for retirement ought to have a last date in place, however won't have a selected financial motive they need to achieve. Similarly, in case you're within the number one saving to set up an emergency fund, you could have a considerable cause of incomes as a superb deal as you may. There's no need to pressure yourself to put a dollar amount on that sort of intention, so long as you trust yourself to prioritize financial savings near making and monitoring your price range.

When you do have unique desires, keep them in thoughts as you decide your investment approach. Make notes of your timeline and purpose monetary financial savings amount to evaluate how a whole lot of a hazard you're inclined to take and slim down your investment alternatives.

Step three. Create a Portfolio

Creating a portfolio will help you bought and oversee your investments. A portfolio is like a group of severa monetary investments. You can frequently display your portfolio and make changes as critical to make sure you're heading inside the proper route to meet your goals. Remember that the market fluctuates frequently, so that you need to preserve a level head if you take a look at in and spot which you lost coins inside the destiny. Know it'll stability out in time and keep tracking it to ensure the business enterprise's inventory isn't plummeting for real motive.

Ideally, you diversify your investments lots that you usually have your money running for you. This method you need to see the whole lot, even when you have unique asset commands, like shares, bonds, and real belongings. You also can diversify your portfolio with the aid of enterprise corporation.

For instance, you should buy stocks in retail companies, engineering companies, and software program manufacturers. While you continue to have a difficult and fast sum of money invested in stocks, you're going to make cash in amazing industries that have numerous risks and payoffs.

This device can help boom your functionality to earn strong returns.

Step 4. Regular Check-Ins

Investing isn't like placing money in a monetary financial savings account and letting it take a seat down down. You want to test in often to make sure they're paying off and retaining you at the proper music for your monetary desires. You can generally regulate your investments, so the more you take a look at in, the faster you may determine if some element isn't running, pull your cash, and spend money on every specific avenue.

Over time, your danger tolerance may alternate and also you'll need to adjust your funding approach. This may additionally moreover take region whilst your timeline changes. The extra you study your portfolio, the higher geared up you are to maintain your earning capability.

Step 5. Stay Informed

Finances are in no manner stagnant. The inventory marketplace fluctuates every day and is drastically impacted with the useful resource of factors going on within the u . S . A . And round the area. You need to stay knowledgeable so that you can decide how positive topics can also additionally impact your investments. You ought to study up on market dispositions, financial tendencies, and investment data. The more , the better knowledgeable you are whilst making funding alternatives.

You can installation Google Alerts for the stock market or precise investment possibilities. You additionally may be part of on line boards wherein distinct investors speak about their thoughts and strategies. Even in case you great have a look at and don't placed up or take part, you're taking in their understanding and the use of it on your advantage.

Investing is a way to make your coins give you the results you want. Compound interest and the inventory market are strategies to allow your bills earn money even as you live your life. Starting early gives you the most time to ensure your cash can make bigger, even in case you only invest a small quantity to begin. With the promise of prolonged-time period rewards, your investing adventure may additionally have a first-rate payoff that units you up for monetary fulfillment.

Activity

Practice on-line making an investment—with out placing your cash at risk. This is a practice interest that will help you enlarge real-existence skills.

Research stocks on-line and think about what groups you'd want to assist. You need to bear in mind many elements of the industrial enterprise business enterprise, along with in the event that they align collectively along with your values and in the event that they have coins-making capability. While you want to manual businesses that rely to you, you moreover may additionally need to be clever and select ones which might be much more likely to gain achievement because of the truth which means that that they'll expand your cash the maximum.

Chapter 5: Learn The Art Of Saving Money

Saving coins really is an artwork—it's something you want to work out and hone over time till you switch out to be a maintain close. As quick as you begin making a dwelling, whether it's an allowance or from a mission, you can begin growing the inspiration of actual behavior that empower you to keep coins. When you store, you have got were given a safety internet that might defend you in case of economic emergencies. You'll have the skills had to discover ways to benefit your financial desires and become sincerely unbiased.

Importance of Saving Money for Teens

Smartphones, drugs, and get proper of entry to to the internet constantly has made immediate gratification the same old for maximum matters. Instant gratification way you get what you want or want as quick as you are searching for it.

For example, you can look up the answer to a query, be aware of music, and contact buddies in only a few seconds collectively collectively with your cellular telephone at your fingertips. However, saving money isn't that clean. It takes time to earn and store cash and staying energy to watch your monetary institution account develop.

While your motive for saving cash may be to establish a nest egg for university or purchase your first domestic, that isn't all you're doing with this method. You're developing robust behavior that help you come to be a responsible character due to the reality you're saving coins in place of spending it as rapid as you earn it.

Acts as a Building Block for Financial Independence

Saving coins acts as a constructing block for financial independence. In truth, you could argue that it's the muse of independence. When you keep cash, you're giving yourself assets you'll want at the equal time as you live in your non-public. Earning coins gives you a extremely good interpretation of the fee of each greenback. Accumulating hard-earned cash allows you experience on top of things and offers you the danger to make sensible choices collectively collectively along with your cash in terms of methods you spend or save it.

When you start strolling, you need to set some financial desires. Think of factors you'd like to hold up to shop for on the aspect of ways a good deal money you'd want to must your economic monetary financial savings account for emergencies or some issue else. Your financial desires also can encompass extra favored terms, like how lots you're inclined to spend on amusing topics every month compared to how masses you deposit into financial savings.

You'll experience a enjoy of fulfillment at the equal time as you keep cash, irrespective of the manner you advise to spend those budget. You'll usually attain new milestones for your financial savings journey, allowing you to hold a tremendous benchmark amount and invest within the large-charge rate price ticket devices you set a reason to shop for.

Gives the Control of Money in the Hands of Teens

Learning a way to keep coins gives you manage of your cash, which leads you to monetary independence. You received't must depend upon your dad and mom to loan you money to shop for belongings you need. You obtained't locate yourself out with friends, not able to join them for dinner because of the fact you don't have your private money and don't want to ask one in each of them to cover your invoice. Financial independence helps you experience confident and mature due to the fact you're able to fund your lifestyles.

The greater you shop, the greater you'll find out about money control. You're already reading about budgeting and funding opportunities just from analyzing this e-book. When you have coins for your account, you'll observe even more approximately hobby charges, investments, and passive earnings. You'll have a chance to get a credit score score card and set up a sturdy credit score score to help you stable loans, belongings, and cars in adulthood. Financial know-how also can guard you from falling for scams that drain your bank money owed, so that you can lessen your pressure tiers and empower you to be extra proactive on the identical time as growing a living alternatives.

Independence is one trouble you'll research from saving coins, however economic protection is also a main perk. You don't want to set prolonged-time period wants to have a purpose to keep; you can keep because you want to understand you've got were given got coins within the bank while you want it. The greater you store, the much less likely you're to spend your cash, looking for things you don't really need.

Chapter 6: There Are Numerous Procedures To Earn Cash On Line

The majority best require a reliable net connection and a laptop or mobile device. These tactics to make coins not handiest don't price lots to begin, but they also will will permit you to paintings on your private from the comfort of your private home.

It isn't always unexpected that extra humans are searching out methods to earn cash on line, given all of these benefits and the increase of eCommerce due to the COVID-19 pandemic.

35 thoughts for being profitable online are compiled in this ebook. We have broken the mind down into lists, one with 10 quick-cash techniques and the opposite with 25 extended-term earning strategies. I desire this text has taught you the way to earn money on-line.

Top 10 Quick Ways to Make Money Online

1.Complete Surveys Online

2. Try out apps and games.

3. Give comments and test the internet websites 4.Investigate Mystery Shopping

five.Selling Second-Hand Goods

6.Promote School Notes

7.Work on Voice-Over

8.Sell Designs and Art

9.Sell Stock Images and Video

10.Execute Micro Jobs

The Top 25 Long-Term Online Money Making Strategies

1 . Make a residing as a digital assistant

2.Apply for Freelance Positions.

3.Invest in Stocks

4.Earn Money Through Blogging

5.Create eBooks

6.Create a Course Online

7. Online university students' tutoring

eight. Provide Services in Digital Marketing

9. Become a journey agent

10. Market Advertising Space

eleven. Participate in an Affiliate Program

12. Launch Email Marketing Campaigns

13. Create a domain for membership

14. Create a 15-net web page app

15. Create a technique board for subscribers

sixteen. Learn to put in writing content material

17. Learn to design pix at age

18. Become net developer

19. Create a Dropshipping Business

20. Create a net internet site for e-commerce

21. Flip and Buy Websites

22. Start a podcast

23. Create a YouTube channel.

24. Turn out to be an influencer

25. Becoming a online game streamer.

Top 10 Quick Ways to Make Money Online With an Internet connection.

Almost anything can be accessed from any device or location. Take a examine my top choices in case you want to earn coins proper away:

1. Complete surveys on-line:

Share your mind on famous survey internet sites for extra cash.

2. Test software application application and video video games:

Provide builders with insights into the person revel in of their software program software.

2. Check out net web sites:

Give human beings feedback on their web sites to reason them to plenty much less tough to use.

four. Consider thriller buying:

Earn coins through writing critiques and sharing your consumer experience.

five. Sell topics which is probably used:

Sell used devices like garments, home device, and vehicles to remove clutter.

6. Sell notes for college:

Popular with students who need to earn extra cash whilst maintaining proper grades.

7. Work on voice-overs:

Utilize your talents as a narrator for audiobooks, trailers, and commercials.

eight. Make paintings and designs a profits:

Accept paintings commissions and marketplace merchandise imparting your designs.

9. Sell snap shots and stock snap shots:

best for videographers and photographers searching for a way of passive income technology.

10. Perform small obligations:

Ideal for people with constrained technical competencies and some unfastened hours.

Let's take a higher have a study those ideas for making money on line and talk approximately how to make your enterprise be triumphant.

1. Stats for Completing Online Surveys approach

Time required for setup: simplest takes a few minutes, and customers pleasant need to create an account.

Age restrict: 13+ to 18+, varies from internet site to internet internet site.

Payment time: varies steady with the minimal amount required to withdraw finances.

Although it could sound too suitable to be actual, you can earn extra cash through taking on line surveys for your spare time.

Participation in surveys for sizeable market research and patron behavior evaluation is paid for thru the usage of many agencies. These surveys assist agencies in making employer choices, which includes which merchandise to launch or wherein classified ads need to be published.

However, now not every body is capable of take surveys on line. Some surveys, as an example, best aim precise demographics, which includes human beings of a particular gender, age, or profession.

The majority of survey net websites have a minimal profits that is relatively low.

You should, as an instance, earn $zero.50 to $three constant with survey. But you may not be capable of cash out except you earn amongst $10 and $25 in typical. Surveys aren't a excellent lengthy-term way to make money on line for the ones reasons.

If you do not thoughts the functionality drawbacks, right right here are a few famous survey net web web sites:

Swagbucks. To get elements, watch movies, play video video games, and whole online surveys. After that, trade them for gift gambling playing playing cards or coins.

Survey addict. By participating in their market surveys, you may assist manufacturers in presenting better items and services.

Online Harris Poll. Participate in a rewards software program by using the usage of responding to survey structures' polls.

QuickRewards. Take surveys, play video video games, watch films, complete offers, or shop online to earn coins via PayPal. To coins out, no minimal quantity is needed.

2. Stats for Testing Apps and Games method

Time required for setup: mins to hours, counting on the length of the game

Age restriction:thirteen-18+

Time body for charge: between a few days and a few months after finishing the sport or its beta version. In 2021, the online game organisation changed into well really worth $178.Seventy 3 billion, up 14.Four% from 2020.

Additionally, video video video games have the most important percent of the global market for virtual media. Consequently, severa possibilities for clients to test video video games and first rate apps and earn coins on line have emerged.

Players in some apps, like Mistplay, are required to finish particular obligations so you can earn forex rewards. These rewards can be exchanged for present playing playing cards or real cash.

Keywords Studios' Global Beta Test Network pays humans to play video video video games earlier than they are released. Real cash prizes can be acquired in different on line video video video games like Givling.

However, structures that use games and apps as a ruse to thieve personal information and economic group account records have to be prevented. Even despite the fact that they offer an clean manner to make cash on line, take a look at critiques to make certain they'll be real first.

3. Stats for test Websites and Provide Feedback approach

Time required for setup: a few minutes; clients usually want to sign on and take a short exercise test.

Age limit: 16 or older to 18 or older, varies through the use of way of net web page

Payment time: after the take a look at, one to two weeks later If you've got got a eager eye for web site design and improvement, you can need to turn out to be a internet net web site tester. It's a first rate manner to get concerned in the internet development enterprise and rapid earn cash.

To check net web sites, you need if you need to expect critically and logically, talk effectively, and be acquainted with the layout and capability of websites. Your test-reporting extremely good and interest prospects may be extra first-rate via those tendencies.

Typically, bills are based totally on the assignment, and fees variety counting on the sorting out techniques and platform coverage.

UserTesting, for instance, offers assessments for $4–$one hundred and twenty. More cash is made with the aid of net website on line testers who participate in stay interviews with customers.

Other marketplaces offer net website attempting out responsibilities as a manner to earn cash on-line:

Ubertesters. A enterprise that uses crowdsourcing to test video video games, cellular apps, and internet internet sites.

Userbrain. A net device for sorting out the client experience of virtual product prototypes and web sites.

Testbirds. Testing the consumer revel in of digital products like health trackers, cellular apps, and online stores

Userlytics. It gives initiatives that focus on reviewing video classified ads similarly to sorting out web web sites and programs.

Trymata. Offers usability exams for websites and mobile apps through recorded movies and written remarks based totally on surveys.

four.Stats for thriller purchasing technique

Time required for setup: a couple of minutes; all users want to do is join up at the net website. Age restriction:sixteen-18+

Time frame for price: varies from industrial corporation business enterprise to business organisation enterprise corporation. If you enjoy purchasing for, turning into a mystery consumer is a notable way to earn extra money.

Mystery customers are hired via retailers and marketplace research corporations to keep at particular places and document on the overall consumer experience. They check product incredible, maintain conditions, and customer support with out the business organisation's personnel know-how.

Remote mystery buying artwork is an possibility. Some jobs, as an example, require assessing the shopping for revel in of a web keep or attempting out the exceptional of a call middle.

The following are a number of the most well-known groups in which human beings can be part of as much as be mystery purchasers:

Force of Market Try out the goods and services of grocery shops, eating locations, pharmacies, or even gasoline station consolation shops with the useful resource of means of having employed.

BestMark. Become an evaluator or discipline representative to assist businesses in improving their organisation practices.

The Secret Shopper Conduct cell smartphone or on-website online issuer evaluations for global organizations.

The portions paid to mystery shoppers variety from organisation to organisation. You can earn among $10 and $25 on not unusual for each pastime you end, get keep of vouchers and present playing cards, or be reimbursed for the topics to procure.

Remember which you need to in no way pay to come to be a mystery patron that allows you to stay far from scams. Additionally, as an impartial contractor, agencies can't compel you to deal with a predetermined large sort of mystery customer assignments.

five. Stats for the Sell Second-Hand Items Method

Time required for setup: as a minimum some hours—customers should be part of up for the website, take snap shots of products, and create listings for them.

Age restrict:16-18+

Time body for price: as soon as each week or every ten days.

Selling or renting out 2nd hand objects is some distinct super manner to make coins and a splendid way to get recommended to start organizing your region. Additionally, due to the fact you're remarkable promoting assets you already very very own, selling used gadgets can be a value-effective preference.

Before list your products on on line marketplaces, take great pics of them after you have got were given compiled an stock. Make a internet net page to host your very own on line hold in case you intend to do this over time.

Clothing is one of the maximum famous commands of used devices. By 2026, it is expected that the second-hand garb agency may have a marketplace fee of $seventy seven billion. As a give up end result, now is a great time to open a 2d hand clothing keep.

The market for secondhand apparel and add-ons is served with the useful resource of many on-line marketplaces. A few examples embody:

thredUP. An online thrift and consignment keep in which you should buy and sell exceptional secondhand garb.

Etsy. A wonderful place to sell vintage or one-of-a-type home made gadgets.

Depop. A properly-favored platform for promoting fashion designer and virtage items like used shoes, rings, and T-shirts.

You should make an entire lot of money online by way of selling used cars, sports activities sports system, furniture, devices, and garments in addition to add-ons. The marketplace for used vehicles inside the

United States professional massive boom in 2021 and is anticipated to stay sturdy in 2023.

eBay, Gadget Salvation, Swap.Com, Reverb, and Fat Llama are some of the remarkable places to sell used items on-line.

6. Stats for the Sell School Notes Method

Time required for setup: minutes to hours, counting on how many notes you upload Age limit: 13 years vintage or older, varies with the aid of manner of net website.

Payment approach: monthly, upon request, or if you have sufficient credit to coins out – varies from net web page to net website online. One of the very satisfactory methods for college kids to make brief cash is to promote copies of school notes.

However, in case you promote college notes, take a look at to appearance which you aren't venture academic misconduct or plagiarism. Don't, for example, communicate approximately upcoming assessments or assignments or distribute material that is protected via copyright.

Selling notes like modules, flashcards, and have a look at courses that provide standard however insightful facts about a topic is the most secure opportunity. Since your notes are actually more have a have a study files, you need to be careful now not to give them as information.

The following are a number of the top notch on line possibilities for earning income by using the use of promoting college notes, further to message boards and network boards for college kids or alumni:

Notes on Nexus They offer a 50% charge on each sale of notes.

NoteXchange. If you turn out to be an associate, you could earn a a hundred% fee even as you promote notes for $5 to $forty or extra.

Notesgen. This India-based totally sincerely platform accepts handwritten notes and presentation slides. It has over 5.Five million users. Study guides fee everywhere from a hundred to extra than 1000 greenbacks.

OneClass. When someone subscribes for your content material, you can get up to 20% of the recurring sales. It prices among $1.8 and $24 for each subscription.

7. Stats for the Voice-Over Work Method

Time required for setup: some hours—you will want to set up your recording device and software software and be part of up for web sites. You need to be as a minimum 18 years vintage.

Payment due: ten days after the project is finished, monthly, or weekly, relying on the net website on-line. Voice-over art work is a first rate way to make cash fast. There isn't any need for an extended-time period strength of mind in voice-over paintings due to the truth maximum jobs are challenge-based totally.

To narrate audiobooks, advertisements, trailers, demonstration films, and audio courses, groups are constantly looking for new voice actors.

The form of task, the duration of the script, and your diploma of revel in all play a characteristic in determining your profits from voice-over work. In america, voice-over artists earn approximately $30 in keeping with hour on not unusual.

However, expert audiobook voice talents can earn as an awful lot as $two hundred in step with finished hour, this is same to the reading time of a e-book.

Creating a profile on a settlement market like Upwork and responding right away to voice-over task classified ads is one of the easiest techniques to get began. A tremendous manner to check the waters and take a look at jobs is to enroll in freelance web web sites.

Alternatively, join up for Voices or ACX, which connect clients with voice actors and authors with audiobook narrators.

A properly voice-over artist is dynamic and flexible. No depend what the hassle is, they are able to deliver a script to lifestyles. A constant narrative voice, wonderful articulation abilties, and the ability to voice numerous characters are crucial for audiobooks.

Check out some pattern scripts to look which area of hobby excellent fits your voice and fashion. Investing in a super microphone and recording software application is a ought to due to the fact generating remarkable audio is vital for this manner. When recording audio samples, strive and decrease historical past noise as an entire lot as possible.

Chapter 7: Stats For Selling Designs And Art Technique

Time required for setup: a few days to three months, relying on how a good deal time you decide to artwork and design

Time frame for price: 5 to seven days after the transaction is completed or every month, relying on the internet internet site online. One of the exceptional methods for artists to make money is to promote digital products.

Place your works on art work marketplaces like ArtStation and DeviantArt. This is a top notch manner to accumulate ability clients and advantage exposure inside the innovative on line community.

Alternatively, you could promote designs and paintings to your very private via a exceptional profits channel like your social media account. Instagram had more than one billion monthly lively clients and Facebook had more than billion as of January 2022. These structures are exquisite for growing publicity because of their big numbers.

If you sell your art work on specific networks, selling on social media is a exquisite way to make coins rapid.

Start selling on Facebook Marketplace, for instance, and sell your products with the resource of interacting with potential clients and becoming a member of corporations. Alternatively, on an account devoted on your paintings, permit the Instagram Shopping characteristic.

Utilizing hashtags, attractive captions, regular artwork posting, interacting with large payments, and following clients with similar hobbies will all assist you growth profits.

It is feasible to make as lots as ninety five% of sales on a marketplace like ArtStation. Selling for your very own social media debts, however, permits you to maintain as plenty as one hundred% of the earnings.

9. Stats for the Sell Stock Photos and Footage Method

Time required for setup: a few days to a few months, depending on how prolonged you spend taking photographs and video.

Age restrict: Time frame for price: each month or as normal with the selected charge time table, which varies from internet web page to net web page. If you are a passionate photographer or videographer, you will likely need to sell inventory pictures and pix to make cash passively. You'll be able to do what you want and make coins at the equal time.

Stock content material material is utilized by many businesses and organisation owners in marketing and advertising campaigns, classified ads, and websites. To make their brand stand out, companies continuously look for novel principles and perspectives further to the same vintage inventory image layout.

You can sell snap shots on a pictures net website on-line. It's also a extremely good concept to list your digital downloads and be part of online marketplaces. You may be capable of get a head begin on growing your private logo at the same time as additionally selling it to capacity customers in this way.

The following are a number of the most well-known web websites for video and stock photographs:

Shutterstock. Includes more than one earning levels which is probably decided thru the every year amount of picture and video licenses.

Images by using the use of Getty range from 15 to forty five percent relying on the exclusivity agreement for the license.

VideoHive. As a part of the larger Envato surroundings, sells inventory motion images. The quantity you are making is inspired through how many gadgets you sell and whether or not or now not you promote absolutely at the platform.

Dissolve. Sells superb inventory motion pictures and pix, charging non-particular members a famous royalty rate of 30% of the net selling fee. Rates which may be made to be had upon request can help distinctive people earn more money.

10. Stats for do Micro Job's Method

Time required for setup: a few minutes – really register on the net website online. Age restrict: 13+ to 18+, varies from internet website to internet site. Payment time: depending on the net web page, up to two weeks after the project is finished, monthly, or upon request. Microjobs are an exquisite way to earn extra cash. A micro activity is a short, quick-time period role that may pay for every challenge completed. From some cents to $50 constant with task, income variety.

Micro jobs are a tremendous way to make cash fast. People can whole more than one obligations of their spare time with some micro jobs, which take a incredible deal much less than an hour to complete.

Because they let you in growing a portfolio and gaining enjoy, they are perfect for freelancers, cutting-edge-day university graduates, and university college students. Blogging, quick translations, information get right of entry to, and administrative duties are the most not unusual on-line microjobs.

Try searching out micro jobs on those internet websites, further to close by means of classifieds:

Fiverr. One of the maximum appreciably used systems for pretty some small duties, collectively with logo format and translation.

Mechanical Turk with the useful resource of Amazon is a outstanding platform for folks that can input and technique information, movies, and snap shots.

Appen. Doing small obligations like transcribe or classify information will allow you to make cash on line.

The top 25 long-time period techniques for making a living on line ultimately.

Now that we have blanketed a number of the pleasant techniques to make coins inside the short term, permit's examine a few lengthy-time period strategies to make cash on-line.

In assessment to the previous segment, the following list of cash-making thoughts might likely necessitate investing a while and money. Still, if you need to decorate your capabilities and work portfolio, you need to think about them.

1.Stats for Becoming a Virtual Assistant approach

Time required for setup: a couple of minutes — actually sign on on the internet website

Age restriction: thirteen+ to sixteen+, varies from net page to internet web site.

Payment time: counting on the platform or enterprise company, up to two weeks after the challenge is completed each month, upon request. A virtual assistant offers guide offerings for person customers or corporations. It's a first-rate manner to make money on-line to end up a digital assistant if you want to plot, installation, or do administrative artwork.

As impartial contractors, many virtual assistants are free to work from home. In addition, there are few preliminary expenses, and you can expect incomes approximately $fifty eight,000 every year.

As a virtual assistant, you'll want to be accurate at writing, speaking, and coping with some time.

It's furthermore important to apprehend the manner to apply challenge control and bookkeeping software program program and gear on-line. Virtual assistants frequently hire a couple of structures, together with Asana, QuickBooks, and Google Drive.

Utilizing on-line systems like Fiverr and Freelancer is the simplest technique of advertising your services. Alternatively, you'll be part of a business enterprise that hires virtual assistants and earn cash thru running with real customers.

2. Stats for Applying for Freelance Jobs approach

Time required for setup: a few minutes—all you need to do is sign on on the internet site. The age restriction levels from 16 to 18, but this varies from net web page to net internet page. Depending on the internet web page, up to 10 days after the mission is completed, monthly, or based totally mostly on the chosen price time table. Freelancing is a fantastic manner to make coins at your private pace. You can choose who you discern for, set your non-public hours, and set your very personal fee.

In the us on my own, there are 50 million freelancers, making it a well-known way to make extra cash. Kelly Vaughn and Muhammad Qasim are of many a success freelancers.

You can offer severa freelance offerings. Video production, translation, internet layout and development, and accounting are maximum of the maximum sought-after freelance abilities.

Sign up for some of the ones freelancing net websites and start looking for paintings:

Upwork. Makes a speciality of enormous initiatives that call for freelancers with particular talents.

Freelancer. Offers opportunities for freelance artwork in more than 1,800 categories.

Guru. Enables human beings and small to medium-sized agencies to post obligations.

Create a web portfolio to beautify your possibilities of touchdown excessive-paying obligations and add on your profile on hobby boards.

Last but not least, check to see that your pricing structure presentations the quantity of effort and time required to finish each undertaking.

three.Stats for Investing in Stocks technique

Time required for setup: Although putting in an account quality takes a few days, gaining knowledge of a manner to exchange stocks can take severa months.

Age restrict: Although the Fidelity Youth Account is open to teenagers aged 13 to 17, it calls for not less than 18 years of age to open it. Approximately agency days after the trade date. Investing in stocks is a notable manner to earn coins passively. Start through the usage of shopping for stocks in a commercial enterprise and then promoting them on the same time as their rate rises.

At first, it could be tough. Thankfully, there are masses of blogs, podcasts, and YouTube channels that provide buying and selling recommendation. They frequently offer inventory buying and selling technique insights, suggestions, and hints.

Collab Fund, A Wealth of Common Sense, and We Study Billionaires are famous getting to know assets.

Stockbrokers' exchange reviews and marketplace news additionally can be beneficial. WhiteBoard Finance and Rayner Teo are of the severa stock searching for and promoting YouTube channels to observe.

Using a transaction-facilitating online stockbroker to buy stocks is the terrific technique. Some of our pinnacle selections are as follows:

E*TRADE. Perfect for lengthy-time period customers searching for a 0-deposit requirement. Users want to, however, fund their debts indoors 30 days.

Ameritrade TD a trading platform with excellent customer support and no commissions.

Investing with Fidelity. Allows buyers with confined capital to take part in the inventory marketplace by way of using imparting fractional stocks.

Schwab, Charles includes international shares and trade-traded budget (ETFs) among particular investment alternatives.

4. Stats for Making Money Blogging approach

Time required for setup: some hours to three days—you want to make a website, installation the format, and post content cloth.

Age limit: Time frame for charge: varies relying on the belongings of earnings. For passionate writers, running a weblog is a superb way to make cash. A lot of humans begin blogs to percent their mind, voice their evaluations, and assemble manufacturers. Say Yes and Anywhere We Roam are a couple of famous blogs.

You are free to start a blog about a few thing. You can find a worthwhile area of interest through studying famous blog thoughts. Travel blogs, food blogs, and ebook blogs are examples of vicinity of hobby blogs.

Advertising, affiliate marketing, sponsoring a logo, and promoting merchandise are the most commonplace techniques to make money blogging.

Find a gap and continuously put up splendid content material material to bring together your aim market for a profitable weblog. It's also vital to use search engine optimization (search engine optimization) and advertising techniques that paintings.

Chapter 8: Stats For Create Ebooks Approach

Time required for setup: Your ebook can be uploaded to the net internet page in a consider of mins, but writing it could take severa years, counting on its assignment and duration.

Age threshold:16-18

Time body for price: 30-forty five days after the month wherein the sale takes vicinity The rise of self-publishing has made eBook publishing available to all and sundry. Since there are not any printing or delivery expenses, it's miles a amazing choice for beginners.

Submit your artwork to a platform for self-publishing in order to make an eBook. Retailers and aggregators are the 2 varieties of publishing businesses. While aggregators distribute books to stores at greater prices, shops sell books right now to customers.

The royalty coverage of the publishing business enterprise will decide how wonderful deal cash you are making from eBooks. For instance, for books which can be bought from the Kindle keep, Amazon Kindle Direct Publishing can pay royalties of up to 70%.

The following are extra eBook publishers and their royalty costs, further to Amazon:

Press from Barnes & Noble. Permits a royalty charge of 70% on eBook earnings.

Writing Life on a Kobo if a ebook charges at least $2.Ninety 9, gives authors 70% of the book's list price.

Apple Publishing for Authors permits authors to acquire 70% of the earnings price of their eBooks.

Smashwords. The largest impartial eBook distributor inside the international, charging a 15% to 18.Five% fee whilst promoting on their website and 10% to other stores and libraries.

Draft2Digital. Allow authors to get hold of 60% of the listing charge of their eBooks as royalties.

Make splendid to thoroughly take a look at your eBook for errors in grammar, typos, and formatting in advance than self-publishing it. Also, you could need to lease a photo fashion fashion designer to help you make an appealing cowl in your eBook.

6. Stats for Creating an Online Course technique

Time required for setup: some days to 3 weeks – you may have to plot your courses, cause them to, submit them, and ship them in for a exceptional take a look at.

Age restriction: sixteen or older to 18 or older, varies with the useful resource of way of website

Payment time: The worldwide eLearning marketplace is anticipated to gain nearly $400 billion by using way of 2026, both days or a month after the sale, month-to-month, or based totally on the chosen price time table (varies amongst websites). It is an first rate time to begin promoting on-line publications if you are an professional in a specific challenge and experience curating academic content material fabric.

Digital guides are available in a number of codecs, consisting of films and smooth PDF downloads. Computer capabilities, virtual marketing, fitness and nicely-being, business and entrepreneurship, making an investment and finance, and private development are all well-known topics for on-line publications.

Selling virtual courses on line can be executed in number one techniques: through becoming a member of an eLearning platform or by using developing an eLearning internet web page. The first is much less hard to do, however the 2d gives you more possibilities to strive awesome codecs and monetization strategies.

A WordPress LMS plugin can be used to make a website for e-studying. Then, sell the guides as virtual downloads or increase a club platform with a paywall.

Consider the following options in case you need to check a few eLearning systems first:

Udemy. Offers severa publications, quizzes, coding sporting sports activities, and talk forums.

Skillshare. High-great for promoting virtual art work and cutting-edge capabilities publications.

Teachable. Spotlight, an eLearning marketplace powered via Teachable and Hotmart, gives creators the opportunity to have their live sports and guides featured there.

Podia. A platform for selling digital downloads, memberships, and on line courses. Courses can be made with the useful resource of customers on their personal or as a drip. They can also package deal deal comparable guides and sell them collectively.

Pathwright. A platform for design, guidance, and studying. Through concrete steps, energetic analyzing is emphasised in its publications.

7. Stats for the Online Tutoring Method

Time required for setup: some days to three weeks to sign up as a train, get approved, make a lesson plan, and set up your tutoring time table.

Age limit: Age variety: 18+ to 21+, varies from website to internet web page. Payment due date: every week, every month, or upon request—varies among websites. If you want to teach however do not want to promote digital guides, you may possibly need to turn out to be a web teach.

Today, many university college students actively are seeking out a long way flung education. Most of the time, independent tutors provide their services thru video conferencing apps like Zoom or Skype and get hold of PayPal bills.

Before deciding on a subject to educate, evaluate your facts. Math, languages, and computing are a few of the most sought-after topics for tutoring. Create learning modules, provide on-name for training, and provide personalised feedback to make coins.

Improve your prices and enhance your credibility as an internet show with the useful useful resource of becoming licensed. Additionally, to ensure easy video communique, installation a reliable net connection previous to wearing out stay classes.

Create a net website online or join an internet tutoring platform whilst you are prepared to promote it your services. The following are 4 well-favored systems for people interested by the internet tutoring company:

Skooli. Lessons can be scheduled in advance or standard whenever you're online.

TutorMe. Matches college students with tutors in line with their options and requirements.

Tutor.Com. Allows tutors primarily based within the United States to teach more than 250 topics to college students ranging in age and schooling diploma.

Preply. Set individualized fees to your services and teach numerous languages.

eight. Stats for Provide Digital Marketing Services approach

Time required for setup: Creating a advertising and marketing provider website excellent takes a couple of minutes if you have already were given a bit portfolio. Age restriction:16-18+

Time body for price: varies relying on the individual case Marketing experts assist business employer proprietors in attracting their intention audiences and growing income standard overall performance.

Offer seek engine marketing offerings to web sites to help them get greater web page visitors, rank higher on searching for engine outcomes pages (SERPs), and generate leads.

By developing and implementing advertising and marketing strategies for the duration of an entire lot of social media structures, you can also provide social media management services. Better goal market interplay and emblem popularity are facilitated by way of the usage of those sports activities.

For higher results, a exceptional social media manager video display gadgets social media statistics, determines a logo's target market, and continues up with dispositions.

There are numerous assets available that will help you in gaining knowledge of WordPress search engine optimization if you use the platform. Take a Google Analytics Academy course or get a certificate in seo from an excellent platform like Semrush Academy to look at more.

You also can take a look at the applicable equipment, principles, and techniques through enrolling in social media advertising and marketing and marketing courses. Coursera has brilliant digital advertising and marketing property, and Udemy has publications on social media marketing and advertising.

Offer your offerings on hobby marketplaces like Fiverr and Freelancer at the identical time as you are geared up to make coins from your abilties. Alternately, for a protracted-time period profession in this vicinity, take into account applying to a marketing company as a digital marketer.

nine.Stats for Becoming a Travel Consultant technique

Time required for setup: in case you have already got tour revel in, up to three hours to installation your very personal net web page or profile on journey representative structures

Age threshold:sixteen-18+

Time frame for fee: varies from case to case due to the growing tourism enterprise and the increased call for for adventure specialists.

For each humans and organizations, adventure experts format the right travel experience. This function is good for people with huge travel enjoy or locals who revel in recommending the exceptional places to make cash on line.

In the united states, a tour representative earns approximately $70,000 yearly as their base revenue. Working from domestic, having a time desk that works for you, and the hazard to adventure are a number of the challenge's advantages.

Learn about well-known software program software program gear for adventure control in advance than you begin your career. To growth your proficiency, you will in all likelihood additionally need to consider enrolling in tourism, hospitality, or distant places language courses.

On your private website, put it on the market your services. Consult with TravelBoecker Adventures and Wanderlust Travel Consultants for thoughts. Alternatively, sign on to artwork as a journey style fashion designer or journey representative on systems like Reco.

10. Stats for the Sell Advertising Space Method

Time required for setup: a couple of minutes if you have already were given a internet internet site that works

Age limit:18+

Time body for price: one of the maximum commonplace approaches to monetize a internet internet web page and earn passive earnings is to sell virtual advertising and advertising location. This can be carried out every month, every week, or 30 days after filing a request or reaching the minimum payout threshold. Since clicks or character impressions are used to degree advertising and advertising and marketing sales, the more interactions you get, the extra cash you could make.

Before buying a space on a internet web website, advertisers bear in mind the content material cloth category, intention marketplace demographics, and devices used by clients. Therefore, enhancing search engine optimization strategies and growing splendid content material fabric are critical.

Sign up for an advert community like Google AdSense and encompass the advert code to your net website to promote ad space. Follow our educational on a way to upload AdSense to WordPress in case you run a WordPress internet site.

However, classified ads ought to not overpower the internet internet site on-line and damage the man or woman revel in. Instead, use a software program software tool referred to as a heatmap to decide out in which to put your classified ads to get the maximum conversions.

You can be part of the subsequent extra advertising and marketing networks:

Adcash. Utilize an anti-block characteristic to get spherical customers' ad blockers and earn extra cash.

PropellerAds. Supports masses of ad codecs, along side push notifications and interstitials.

Media.Net. Gain access to the Yahoo! Search engine's Bing Network for commercials with key phrases in thoughts.

Carbon. A remarkable choice for advertisements based totally totally on generation and layout.

eleven. Stats for join an Affiliate Program Method

Time required for setup: a few days to sign on and get universal if you have already have been given a platform

Age restriction: 16-18+

Time body for charge: more than one times in line with month, 30 to 60 days after the stop of the month, relying at the internet site. Another wonderful manner to make cash online is to sign up for an accomplice marketing software program software.

As an associate, you could promote companies, merchandise, or offerings on your platform and earn a fee. When someone makes a purchase after clicking on an companion hyperlink, you could attain part of the sales.

Affiliate marketing and advertising can deliver in loads to tens of masses of bucks for bloggers. The precise profits will depend on what number of associate programs they participate in and how many human beings take a look at the blog.

Join associate advertising and marketing programs which might be appropriate in your corporation. Consider becoming an accomplice, as an instance, if you have a blog approximately technology and web websites.

The following are a number of the most worthwhile accomplice packages:

Associates of Amazon. Considered one in every of the biggest companion networks, with charge expenses of up to 20%.

BeRush. This software is a amazing desire for content material fabric material marketers because it pays a flat $two hundred commission for every Semrush sale.

Affiliate of CJ. A popular preference for friends who want to art work with massive, famous manufacturers and function set up systems.

Partner Network for eBay. An terrific region to start for associates of all degrees and niches, with price charges starting from one to 4 percent.

Program for Affiliates at Tripadvisor high-quality for journey agency associates. It gives publishers with as a minimum 50% of the hotel reserving companions' rate.

Programs for pals of GetResponse a platform that gives friends within the advertising quarter with one-time and routine commissions.

Affiliate advertising, like each exceptional enterprise version, requires trial and mistakes. Choosing the incorrect place of hobby, creating low-pleasant content material material, and ignoring website performance are some of the most common mistakes in accomplice advertising.

Use AffiliateWP in case you private a commercial enterprise and need to quick set up an associate advertising and advertising and marketing software.

An admin dashboard, real-time reporting, an integrated payouts issuer, and customizable emails are a number of the useful associate management functions of the AffiliateWP WordPress plugin.

12. Stats for release Email Marketing Campaigns method

Time required for setup: If you've got already were given a internet website online, it'll take everywhere from a few days to 3 weeks to bring together the e-mail list and create the campaigns.

Age threshold: sixteen+

Time body for rate: more as a manner of generating leads and galvanizing sales conversions than as a right away supply of income. By 2025, the considerable sort of e-mail clients is anticipated to exceed 4.5 billion. As a end result, e-mail advertising will continue to be effective at changing audiences into customers and generating leads.

Chapter 9: Creating A Membership Website Method

Time required for setup: up to three weeks to create the best of a kind club stages and content material cloth.

Age limit:18+

Time body for price: varies primarily based completely mostly on the selected price gateway. Creating a club internet website online is any other excellent way to make cash on-line on a platform you are making your self.

Through subscription plans, membership internet sites make coins with the useful resource of selling get right of entry to to specific content cloth. You can divide contributors' privileges and decide which content material cloth they may be able to get admission to with a tiered membership tool.

Because people are required to renew their plans which will preserve their get right of get admission to to privileges, the subscription gadget generates a everyday sales flow.

A membership net web web page will will let you gather a emblem via fostering a functionality patron base for upselling.

Take perception from quite a few place of interest membership net websites even as designing your very own. The Magnetic Memory Method, as an instance, places an emphasis on self-improvement. In the meantime, Smart Blogger offers advice on content fabric advent and blogging.

Start constructing the club internet website as soon as you have got got diagnosed a market section that hobbies you. WordPress is the maximum truthful technique. The crucial equipment to create plans and acquire online payments are supplied via numerous beneficial club plugins.

14.Stats for Making an App approach

Time required for setup: a few weeks to severa months

Age restriction:18+

Time frame for fee: varies relying at the scenario. Developing an app is one of the pleasant techniques to take advantage of the fast digitalization of cellular devices. Making paid apps or promoting them to unique corporations are strategies to make money online. Instead, you can launch a free app and make money from classified ads and in-app purchases.

It's additionally a excellent manner to make extra cash and discover ways to code and assemble web web sites. Numerous newbie-quality cellular app builders are to be had for those with little to no coding revel in:

Pie Appy. This app builder guides you via the arrival of a client-fine app in just three clean steps. The monthly fees range from $16 to $60 in line with app.

AppInstitute. An app builder that makes it clean to create cellular apps without expertise coding for owners of busy small corporations. Monthly costs range from $fifty nine to $340.

Mobincube. An smooth-to-use app builder that permits the four-step launch of an app. In addition to the paid plans, it gives a free one. The annual prices of the top class plans range from €35.88 to €1,199.88.

Before growing your app, research the marketplace and your competition. Submit your app to the App Store or Google Play Store while you're finished and appearance beforehand to it to be legal. Finally, promote and monetize your app.

15. Stats for Creating a Subscription Job Board method

Time required for setup: a few days to a few months for growing the approach board net net page and selling it to ability employers and venture seekers.

Age limit:18+

Time body for price: varies relying on the chosen price gateway. Job boards have a large market functionality because greater employers are hiring on-line.

With a virtual way board, there are crucial techniques to make cash online. The first choice is to provide employers with space to put it on the market method openings through renting it out. The second preference is to offer system seekers paid membership get right of entry to to one in every of a type assignment listings.

Employers pay a top rate rate for pinnacle elegance hobby post placements on popular technique board web sites like ZipRecruiter, Indeed, and Glassdoor. The posting period, in-intensity company information, or opinions are some of the elements that maximum of these web sites use to decide their pricing plans.

Using a WordPress way board plugin is the maximum honest approach for developing this shape of website. WP Job Manager, for instance, gives equipment for seamlessly submitting and managing manner listings.

Also, you will possibly need to recall installing a club plugin to control who can see pastime postings.

16. Stats for Become a Content Writer approach

Time required for setup: a few days to a few weeks – before approving you as a author, a few customers or businesses request a writing sample.

Age restrict:18+

Time body for price: one of the notable techniques to make cash on line is to end up a content material material creator—both every week or on request—relying at the internet site online. Writing content material may be a profitable detail procedure or a full-time, faraway process that may pay spherical $60,000 consistent with one year on commonplace.

This career path may also moreover furthermore necessitate search engine optimization understanding in addition to writing competencies. When strolling with a content material material control gadget (CMS) like WordPress, being familiar with the basics of HTML and CSS also can be beneficial.

In order to show off their writing abilities and paintings portfolios, many content material writers have websites. Monetizing your weblog is every other manner to make coins on line if it succeeds.

Try your exact fortune on approach forums like Fiverr and Freelancer, in which you can discover an entire lot of art work as a agreement content material cloth author. Alternatively, for consistent employment, be a part of a content material writing business organisation.

The following are some of the first-rate content material cloth writing groups to art work with:

Verblio. Gives a big range of content fabric fabric types, together with press releases and weblog posts.

SEOButler. Seeks freelance writers primarily based absolutely within the US and UK.

Express Authors employs writers and editors to collaborate with a massive international clients.

Textbroker. Permits US residents to write down one-of-a-kind custom content gigs with free registration, adaptable time control, and weekly bills.

17. Stats for Becoming a Graphic Designer method

Time required for setup: a few minutes to 3 days; a few websites will permit you to upload your paintings and find out initiatives whilst you be a part of up at the customer or the net page. Graphic format is every other high-paying career this is absolutely really worth pursuing. The average base profits is round $fifty 8,000 constant with yr. It's a notable way to make cash on line for innovative people.

Learn the vital skills and pick out a layout robust factor. Color concept, typography, and layout software program like Adobe Illustrator or CorelDRAW are all vital capabilities for a logo clothier. To get you started out, there are numerous layout publications to be had on severa eLearning systems.

The nice websites for picture layout gigs online are as follows:

DesignCrowd. Gives a extensive variety of initiatives, including the format of billboards, web web sites, and symbols.

Minty. Best for expert artists trying to find layout responsibilities with contracts which might be mechanically generated.

We make money working from home. Find masses of jobs in a ways off design.

99designs. Offerings in superb picture layout for merchandise, clothing, web sites, apps, agencies, and marketing.

18. Stats for Developing Websites technique

Time required for setup: some days to a few weeks to apply for on-line developer positions if you already recognise a manner to code. Age restriction: Time frame for rate: varies depending on the character. The annual base sales for a agreement internet developer is approximately $80,000. Additionally, employment of net developers and virtual designers is anticipated to upward push with the aid of 23% among 2021 and 2031. Therefore, that is an super time to go into the business enterprise.

Choosing a specialization in internet improvement is the first step in turning into an internet developer. This will assist you stand happy along with your opponents and prevent cash, time, and attempt.

Learn to code after deciding on a discipline of study. There are severa courses and internet net web sites that would assist you:

BitDegree. Gives scholarships and courses for every novices and specialists.

Coursera. Provides certified publications and specializations thru partnerships with more than two hundred universities and companies.

Codecademy. Ideal for novices who select short, interactive instructions.

Udemy. There are numerous on-call for language guides to pick from.

Participating in a coding boot camp like Alchemy Code Lab or Rithm School will let you red meat up your profession if you want to artwork inside the internet development organization.

Chapter 10: Drop Shipping Business Method

Time required for setup: it'll take everywhere from a couple of minutes to a few days to set up the net website online and find carriers. Time frame for rate: varies based totally totally on the chosen price gateway. Dropshipping is a B2C agency version wherein customers sell items thru an internet shop and rely upon a 3rd-birthday celebration provider to manner and satisfy orders. Because you do no longer want to worry approximately transport and stock, it's far less difficult than a latest eCommerce save.

Choosing an opening and an eCommerce platform are the equal for beginning a dropshipping organisation as they are for beginning a regular online save. The primary distinction lies inside the fact that dropshippers should additionally find out the right supplier. In fact, the remarkable of the suppliers should make or damage the organization.

Here are some websites that assist you to connect with dependable carriers to get you started out out:

Spocket. You can pick from masses of providers global and enjoy smooth integration with Shopify and WooCommerce.

Modalyst. Make your online save a group of products from pretty some worldwide vendors. Set costs with the aid of manner of the usage of using the platform's earnings calculator.

SaleHoo. Explore loads of vetted providers at some stage in pretty a few product lessons. Take a take a look at its discussion board for recommendation on dropshipping.

20. Stats for Building an eCommerce Website method

Time required for setup: some hours to three days – you need to make a internet site, listing your products, make inventory, and set up tax and delivery Time frame for fee: varies counting on the chosen rate gateway. One of the nice strategies to make cash is to promote merchandise on line. Due to its blessings, greater physical stores are turning to eCommerce.

eCommerce shops not handiest have a much broader marketplace achieve but also require decrease startup charges. Since you won't want a couple of retail places, you could shop cash on operational prices.

Decide on the shop's place of interest earlier than beginning a web shop. If you are not remarkable, searching at well-known merchandise can assist making a decision which ones to sell.

Making an internet shop has in no manner been less tough manner to the recognition of eCommerce structures. Because it will have an effect on the general enjoy of both you and your customers, choosing the right platform is important.

The following is a listing of the 4 most effective eCommerce platforms for growing a web save:

Builder of internet web web sites with Hostinger. A internet web page builder designed for beginners that gives severa AI-powered system to assist with commercial agency operations in addition to free topics.

WooCommerce. WooCommerce is a WordPress-based certainly open-supply eCommerce platform with all the skills you need to assemble your dream maintain.

PrestaShop. The device for product control and analytics on this eCommerce software program software are robust.

Shopify. A well-known preference for constructing online enterprise net sites that consist of seek engine advertising and marketing and abandoned cart healing system.

Consider packaging, shipping, stock, and warehousing on the same time as developing a marketing strategy.

You may additionally moreover moreover require a enterprise enterprise license, relying on your agency model and area. Certificates of registration, permits from the authorities, every community and federal, and a earnings tax permit are examples of these.

21. Stats for the Buy and Flip Websites Method

Time required for setup: among a few months and some years

Age restriction:18+

Time body for rate: varies from case to case Websites for purchasing and promoting are distinctly sincere. Optimize the content fabric of a bought internet net web page for engines like google like google and yahoo like google, generate sales, and then promote it for a earnings.

Anyone who enjoys website design, improving seo, and enhancing client experience will discover this to be an outstanding challenge for being profitable.

Knowing which internet web sites to buy and put money into is vital because not all internet web sites may be precious in the future. Choosing those which can be already bringing in customers and money is a first rate rule of thumb. Additionally, net web sites with a well-known area of interest and an high-priced area name are plenty less complex to sell for extra money.

Some marketplaces for buying net sites encompass the subsequent:

Flippa. Lets in humans from anywhere inside the international to shop for and sell internet web web sites or domains in pretty a few niches.

Latona's. Using quite a few filters, browse sale-associated net sites and online stores.

Flippers of Empire. Sells internet web sites that make money and feature month-to-month earnings starting from hundreds to loads of lots of bucks.

SideProjectors. A platform in which digital duties like web sites, e-trade stores, apps, and domain names can be bought and provided.

In order to keep away from making a horrible website funding, there are some subjects to preserve in mind.

The first is to inquire approximately the net website online's contemporary-day monetization strategies, profits record, and evidence of concept. Then, have a look at the website website online site visitors's assets and quantity. These are amazing signs of the capacity of a internet website online.

In addition, it's miles a awesome concept to inquire approximately any problems with the net website on line and determine why the actual proprietor is selling it. Last however no longer least, check the history of the seller and keep away from shopping for websites from anonymous brokers.

22. Stats for Make a Webcast

Strategy method

Arrangement time: as tons as half of of a month to enroll in on a diploma, set up your difficulty, and format sound equipment and programming

Age threshold:13+ to 18+, changes for the duration of locales

Season of installment: adjustments depending upon pay belongings like promotions and sponsorships

Beginning a webcast is one of the most useful internet-based totally totally business employer thoughts. The quantity of world digital recording target market members has prolonged continuously at some level inside the course of latest years. It's projected to stretch round 500 million target marketplace members by way of manner of 2024.

A PC or mobile cellular phone with an implicit mouthpiece is sufficient to begin a virtual recording. Be that as it is able to, we advocate putting assets into valid sound gear and programming to in addition increase recording top notch.

All you actually need is a topic to talk about and draw in relational skills. You can also need to make a digital recording approximately any element, from economic hints to actual wrongdoing.

Subsequent to recording and changing the initial no longer many episodes, find out a webcast facilitating diploma to distribute them at the net. Probably the exceptional ones are Buzzsprout, Resound, and Anchor.

Most digital recordings essentially supply in coins from sponsorships. Once your virtual recording has drawn the following, remember pursuing introduction workplaces like Podfly or Pacific Substance to broaden your photograph, high-quality, and crowd reap.

Make a element to enhance the digital broadcast thru virtual amusement and exceptional ranges, as for your very own internet web page on line. A net recording trouble be counted and a legitimate player can help with supporting the virtual broadcast's photograph person and discoverability.

23. Stats for start a YouTube Channel Strategy technique

Arrangement time: a couple of moments simply to make the channel, but handing over recordings can take anywhere from multiple hours to multiple months

Age restriction: 13+ to make a channel, but 18+ to participate in Google AdSense

Season of installment: constantly

Running a YouTube channel is a well-known technique for bringing in coins on the net. As the most essential video-sharing level round the region, it has a crowd of two billion a month to month dynamic clients.

There are various approaches of bringing in coins from a YouTube channel. The preliminary step is pursuing the YouTube Accomplice Program to guarantee you are certified for variation.

The most famous approach for bringing in cash is through selling. Elective version strategies include channel enrollments, Super Visit, Super Stickers, merchandise, sponsorships, and YouTube BrandConnect.

YouTube has many forms of specialty video content material cloth cloth, from gaming responses to on a daily basis video blogs. For instance, our YouTube channel Hostinger Institute offers internet site on line related video educational sports.

To enlarge a YouTube channel, you need to distribute content cloth every time to create perspectives and assemble a crowd of people. Putting assets right into a super virtual digital camera and converting programming can further develop video amazing and entice extra watchers.

Remember to rehearse YouTube Web optimization. This includes which includes essential watchwords and labels to the video titles and improving video portrayals for internet indexes.

Beside being an incredible technique for bringing in coins net primarily based, beginning a YouTube channel can assist a brand. YouTube recordings can produce leads and assist with diverting visitors in your internet internet site on line. Recordings likewise provide a better yield on assignment than static photos, making them an incredible promoting instrument.

24. Stats for exchange proper right into a Computer assignment Decoration Technique approach

Arrangement time: a couple of moments to make a document, but installing your stay streaming hardware, programming, and content material material can also additionally require up to more than one days

Age component: 13+, but a degrees limit version to 18+ clients

Season of installment: continually

Streaming has been required off within the beyond couple of years, growing a everyday of round 2 million ordinary watchers on Jerk by myself.

It's an incredible rewarding concept in the occasion which you're amazing at messing spherical and recognize being in advance than a virtual digital digicam. You can pass for multiple hours all of sudden and hook up with your crowd to cultivate a experience of the nearby region.

Web based definitely ranges like Jerk, YouTube, and Facebook provide companion packages, allowing decorations to famend marketing earnings and tips from their crowd. Computer endeavor decorations can likewise bring in coins from logo preparations, sponsorships, and product deals.

How an entire lot coins you could make is based upon your following's length. For example, the Canadian decoration Cover has an predicted conventional belongings of $8-$12 million and 10 million+ Jerk devotees.

25. Stats for end up a Force to be reckoned technique

Arrangement time: multiple moments simply to make a record on a web-based totally genuinely amusement level, but constructing your crowd would likely require months

Age limit: 13+

Season of installment: differs depending upon pay property like promotions and sponsorships

The constant ascent of net-based totally amusement has settled on powerhouse selling a well-known choice to usher in coins at the internet.

Like offshoot advertising and marketing and advertising, corporations pay forces to be reckoned with to show off their gadgets and administrations. The number one assessment is forces to be reckoned with anticipate to influence people' purchasing options in place of definitely bringing leads.

Like decorations, how thousands cash powerhouses make basically is based upon their following.

The maximum basic additives of being a beneficial powerhouse are growing an character brand and becoming a definitive voice indoors your strong element. This will help with drawing in supporters and publicists.

Albeit severa forces to be reckoned with are on Instagram, you can make the maximum top notch tiers like YouTube and Twitter to bring together a following and make numerous sorts of content material.

Realize which content material cloth sorts flip out exceptional for every degree. TikTok, for example, is marvelous for folks who need to make viral recordings.

Rhett and Connection from Great Legendary Morning and Andrew Rea from Babish Culinary Universe are a part of the extensively diagnosed forces to be reckoned with growing their professions on YouTube.

Instructions to Pick the Most powerful Way to Bring in Cash On the net

Subsequent to figuring out each of the 35 one-of-a-kind strategies at the exceptional manner to usher in coins on the internet, now could be the perfect time to restrict your choices.

Everything being equal, a excellent many human beings can't address multiple alternatives. To help you with pursuing a desire, study the accompanying variables:

Exertion. Consider the time you may spend installing and investigating the brand new pursuit and whether or not or no longer or no longer you have the crucial competencies or experience.

Cost. Gauge whether or no longer you've got got the monetary plan to begin the web-based absolutely completely employer.

Interest. Try not to pick a concept because it appears to be a easy method for bringing in cash quick. It's vital to pick an enterprise you're sincerely inspired via.

Potential. Perceive the monetary functionality of the picked concept and whether or not it thoroughly may be effective over the long haul.

www.ingramcontent.com/pod-product-compliance
Lightning Source LLC
Chambersburg PA
CBHW071444080526
44587CB00014B/1985